ALSO BY MONDO SECTER

Passionate Zen Cooking: The Art of New Japanese-Western Cuisine (with Ari Tomita)

THE
I CHING
HANDBOOK
DECISION-MAKING
With and Without Divination

MONDO SECTER

North Atlantic Books
Berkeley, California

Published by
North Atlantic Books
P.O. Box 12327
Berkeley, California 94712

Printed in the United States of America

Cover and book design: © Jan Camp

Cover and frontispiece brush art: © Mondo Secter

New Trigram Symbols, © 1993 Mondo Secter

Cover Sho (brush writing) and Hexagram Calligraphy: Ari Tomita

Author photo: Dave Bene

For more information on research on the I Ching by the author, go to:
artazzen.com/iching

The I Ching Handbook is sponsored by the Society for the Study of Native Arts and Sciences, a nonprofit educational corporation whose goals are to develop an educational and crosscultural perspective linking various scientific, social, and artistic fields; to nurture a holistic view of arts, sciences, humanities, and healing; and to publish and distribute literature on the relationship of mind, body, and nature.

North Atlantic Books' publications are available through most bookstores. For further information, call 800-337-2665 or visit our website: www.northatlanticbooks.com.

Substantial discounts on bulk quantities are available to corporations, professional associations, and other organizations. For details and discount information, contact our special sales department.

Library of Congress Cataloging-in-Publication Data
Secter, Mondo, 1941-
 [I Ching clarified]
 The I Ching handbook : decision-making with and without divination /
by Mondo Secter.
   p. cm.
Originally published: I Ching clarified. Boston : Charles E. Tuttle Co., © 1993.
 ISBN 1-55643-415-4 (pbk.)
 1. Yi jing. 2. Divination—China. I. Title.
 PL2464.Z7 S43 2002
 299'.51282--dc21
                                                            2002009637
                                                            CIP

1 2 3 4 5 6 7 8 9 / 06 05 04 03 02

This book is dedicated to that which sets us free . . . in memory of Joseph and Gwen Secter who fostered an open mind, embracing uninhibited inquiry, a joy of learning, passion for exploration, and an attitude respecting and honoring all cultural traditions.

The Journeyer

I am traveling
and unraveling
        colored threads
        and watch the patterns
shift and disappear

a jester in the flow
discovering
        i do not know
        much of anything and find
i do not mind

the reasons for most everything
        i do
        are not the ones
        i thought they were

so now and then deferring
in submission
        to my intuition
        i discern with inner sight
that everything turns out all right

m.s.

Contents

Part One

PART TWO

LIST OF FIGURES

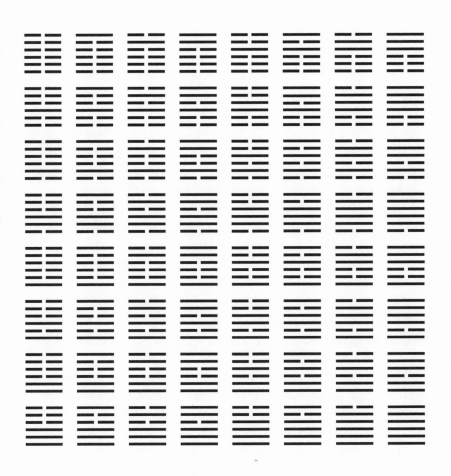

Figure 1. Fu Xi Square

An ancient binary arrangement of the sixty four hexagrams
attributed to Fu Xi, the legendary founder of Chinese culture, but
credited to the Neo-Confucian philosopher Shao Yung (1011–1077).
Through his understanding of the I Ching, he saw numerical
progression as the underlying universal principle.

Acknowledgments

I am greatly indebted to Richard Wilhelm and Cary Baynes for the Wilhelm/Baynes I Ching, which started me on this lifelong journey in 1968. I am equally grateful to John Blofeld, whose more portable translation was my regular companion during the years I traveled and sojourned in Asia. Their books lifted me to a place where I felt comfortable writing this book in 1981. I had the opportunity to spend a few hours alone with Mr. Blofeld in the mid-1980s, following a talk he gave at the University of Hawaii.

I thank Wolfgang and Monika Juneman who saw the merit of publishing this book in German in 1984. They have remained friends ever since. Also, I thank Mike Kerber, who published the book at Tuttle.

I am sincerely grateful to Colleen Murphy, my friend, partner, and companion during the seminal years of this book's gestation. I wrote the outline and notes for this book in Paul Mitchell's Honolulu studio at the time he was starting a hair product line. A true friend, he generously gave me the use of his "island" car and his spacious studio during my extended stays between trips to Asia.

Lastly, I thank Ari Tomita, who has shared my life and enriched it immeasurably from the time this book was first published in German eighteen years ago. Ari is a classically trained master brush artist from Tokyo, who graciously created the Chinese writing on the cover and the characters for the hexagram names.

PREFACE TO THE SECOND EDITION

After completing this book in 1983, I was invited to study Chinese religion and philosophy at the University of Hawaii, where I eventually received an M.A. During that time I spent a year in central China, teaching Western culture and learning to understand a Chinese perspective.

The new chapter in this book is loosely based on my doctoral research. It introduces an aspect of Chinese wisdom with practical benefits for personal decision-making and professional problem-solving. As technology speeds up changes in communication, transportation, and information processing, the acceleration confronts us with more information and greater complexity that we are required to deal with in a shorter span of time. This puts us under greater pressure to think, act, and respond quickly. However, our education and upbringing have not prepared us properly or adequately to manage the ongoing experience of rapid change.

The *I Ching,* when used appropriately, is a useful model for managing change in the 21st century. It provides a way of correlating experiences, thoughts, perceptions, and impressions to trigrams and hexagrams that we begin to recognize and organize as archetypal patterns according to their deep similarities, not their surface differences.

The *I Ching* is a non-linear model in which change is the norm and to be expected. It discloses the rules of change and how to deal with problematic situations by amplifying the positive and managing that which is other than positive. It is a guide to achieving the beneficial and avoiding that which is detrimental, to transforming the things we can, and optimizing the rest. In these ways it provides a tool for obtaining a greater measure of direction and control over probable outcomes.

Although the book was written in English, it was first published in German in 1984 with the title *Das I Ging Handbuch* (*The I Ching Handbook*), followed later by the English edition, *I Ching Clarified*. This new edition has two changes from the original book plus some minor corrections.

1. I added a chapter on using the *I Ching* for decision-making without the divination that is traditionally part of the *I Ching*. This approach shows how to define or frame situations according to two trigrams. These are used to form a hexagram that provides a context for the situation or problem at hand. This chapter expands upon my doctoral work that adapts the principles of yin and yang to defining organizational culture. The model describes eight organizational types and identifies areas of compatibility and conflict between parties considering cross-cultural partnerships or collaborations. In all cases, the hexagrams serve as the starting points for managing positive change.

2. The second change relates to the set of eight hexagram cards I invented in 1975. These are described in the back of the book along with information on obtaining a set. In my own work with the *I Ching*, I have found the cards invaluable for understanding the principles of transformation and change.

I hope this new edition will contribute to deepening your understanding of yourself by revealing the nature of change and the fundamental, interconnected, and mutually informing character and nature of things.

Consider the text of the hexagrams, then set the words aside. Try to understand their meanings through the traditional and new symbols, and discover their relevance in the quiet of your mind or heart. In this sense, the hexagrams are similar to paradoxical Zen koans, those perplexing verbal conundrums that cannot be resolved intellectually, but only through direct internal experiencing.

Mondo Secter, *May, 2002*

FOREWORD

Since antiquity the *I Ching, Book of Change,* has signified many things. It is an embodiment of a system of primordial insights into the cosmology of reality of which man is a refined replica as well as its potential self-consummation. The implicit philosophy of the *I Ching* has been put to many explicit uses for practical life. Divination is clearly one of the major explicit uses of the *I Ching.*

When people think of the practical use of the *I Ching* as a divinatory book they may perhaps forget the pristine insights of its cosmo-philosophy. When more recent scholars came to discover the great philosophical system in the *I Ching* they tended to forget or condemn its meaningful use in divination. Nonetheless, both the theoretical and the practical aspects of the *I Ching* tradition persist and equally command our respect and attention.

Apart from discovering that the *I Ching* may contain the genetic code and such other scientifically coded relationships as those between elementary particles, the *I Ching* presents itself in another important role. This is the role of synthesizing East and West philosophy and thus providing a foundation for inter-cultural communication.

As the complex nature of the *I Ching* and its corresponding multifaceted and multi-leveled usefulness gradually unfolded, the dazzling and perhaps wondering or curious Western mind needed a good, simple and logical introduction to this book. Can the *I Ching* be simply and logically introduced? The answer is that there is nothing in the *I Ching* that prevents such an enterprise from being done. To take on such an effort requires only a good, logical mind that is well motivated to study the *I Ching* and an intuitive excitement over the importance of the *I Ching*. Although many people have attempted this task before, there is a growing need for a new form of presentation of the *I Ching*.

I met with Mondo Secter in 1980 when he came to see me and discuss his work on the *I Ching*. He has studied it for many years on his own and has sought enlightenment from some Chinese Ch'an masters and teachers learned in various aspects of traditional Chinese culture and philosophy. I am very impressed by the fact that Mr. Secter is able to simplify the divination process with the creation of his *I Ching* Cards, and a New Coin Method in harmony with the Yarrow Stalks. These relate to his introductory work on the *I Ching*.

This is a significant beginning for a new era of *I Ching* research, especially meaningful for those who have little or no prior knowledge of the *I Ching* and who wish to appreciate how it can be useful based upon fundamental insights into the nature of reality of both man and nature.

Having done research and study into the history and philosophy of the *I Ching* for over twenty years, and having given numerous advanced seminars at universities in both the East and the West, *I take this opportunity to welcome this well-timed and good introductory book to the Western reader. Not only do I welcome it, but I highly recommend it based on its merits.*

Dr. C.Y. Cheng, *1993*
Professor of Chinese Philosophy, University of Hawaii
Founder and Editor, Journal for Chinese Philosophy
Co-Founder, International Society for I Ching *Studies*

Preface

The modern world has been deeply imprinted by three one-sided (dualistic) determinations; in modern terms *programmings:*

I. Twenty-five hundred years ago — after Herakleitos — the polar view of the world disappeared, owing to the *patriarchy* that represented only the masculine side of the human race.

2. As a result, all attempts to grasp (comprehend) reality became one-sided, materialistic and rational, confined to *outer* (external) graspable objects, which were missing (deprived of) the *inner,* transcendent, aesthetic, ethical, and social aspect of things.

3. The only thing that mattered was *exact* research, which took over. It is not surprising, then, that the other (holistic) world became relegated to the shadow existence of religious superstition, which, lacking a holistic and forceful (energetic) over all structure, fragmented into the mere shadow of holy existence in the form of pale faith-oriented religion.

Mysticism, occultism, spiritism, and astrology were unable to form a universally valid counterbalance to religious faith. In astrology the gulf between the actual planet Venus and the attributes of the goddess Venus remained unabridged and hypothetical, far-removed from any exact theory.

The way to overcome or transcend materialism, however, should be clearer as a result of the work of Einstein. For Heisenberg and Planck, for whom matter dissolved into energy, the concept of information moved across to a place where it became replaced by the concept of transcendence. For them the experimenter became a necessary component of the experiment within the totality of a universal field theory of elemental quanta and elementary particles. Universal polarity in the atom as well as in electricity and magnetism would, however, shortly become something scientifically self-evident and taken for granted.

Now we see that the earlier polar and holistic teachings are recovering ground on what can only be called the disastrous splitting or division of the spirit. These teachings are generating quite an unexpected interest and significance. The takeover of rational patriarchy by a *masculine/feminine becoming human or male-female genesis* with full representation of the hitherto suppressed and repressed female side of our humanity seems necessary in order to alleviate the many distresses mankind is experiencing in all areas and aspects of life.

And now in the late twentieth century an ancient, primarily polar, holistic world-teaching comes forth that integrates (albeit only partially and with a veneer of patriarchy) body, soul, and spirit. This universal formula, which has lain in the shadowy drawers of sinologists for thousands of years and appeared as an oracle on tables at fairs and carnivals, now comes to light as a star of the first magnitude, enlightening reality.

This is the *Yijing, (I Ching)*, the culmination of Chinese thought concerning spirit and nature. This book offers and represents:

1. A mathematical, computer-analog sixty-four-triplet code for all phenomena

2. A teaching of the qualities of these unities, read as sixty-four hexagrams, represented as numbers embodying physical, ethical, and social values simultaneously — not unlike those

discovered by Pythagoras, but forgotten by the rationalistic philosophers

3. The incalculable, innumerable relations of these quanta to each other, flashing in every possible combination

4. The reaction of all these phenomena, values, and functions in a cosmic consciousness, in, an *Akashachronik* or Akashic record, of which each single numerical unit represents a quantum or tiny particle of this cosmic totality and world consciousness

5. Through this totality of *inter-connexions* (total inter-connectedness) in which the part always represents the whole and the whole the part, every part is just the whole (which it represents) structured according to magnetic and electric polarity. Here there obviously arises a possibility that is as surprising as it is natural from the perspective or position of (each person's) individual I, the total current situation can be rendered visible and experiential

This kind of exact experiment defied and refused to comply with the hitherto uncontested fetish of *exact* research. Because as a theory it did not provide objective proof of its effectiveness, it has until now been deprecatingly misunderstood as an *oracle*.

Precisely because the *Yijing* could not be integrated into a Western world-view on a materialistic, philosophical, or religious level — this in spite of the fact that it had a binary mathematics 5,000 years before Leibniz and anticipated computer language — it now manifests as a system of order with the characters of a field or world theory-or even a world formula!

A remarkable *proof* for the universal validity, and effectiveness, and, above all, the dynamic power of this cosmic field (*Yijing* system) was provided by the discovery of the DNA genetic code valid for all life. In a revelation totally surprising to biologists unfamiliar with the *Yijing* and to experts in the *Yijing* unacquainted with modern biology, this code which is the same for plants and animals including human beings — is a sixty-four-triplet code exactly analogous to the sixty-four-triplet system of the *I Ching*.

Almost simultaneously it dawned on several people that this DNA and the *Yijing* represented the appearance of a single world code or programming system of all life. The first was Dr. Marie Louise von Franz; the second, the modest personage of a country doctor, the writer of this introduction; and later, Professor Gunter Stent of the U.S.A. and the sinologist Dr. Frank Fiedeler.

The sixty-four program-unities of biology, the *codons* of DNA, are turning out to be the bearers of psychical, spiritual, and even ethical values and significances. This discovery appears to overcome altogether the split between the natural and mental sciences, and consequently the both *ancient-and-new* unity of spirit (code) — soul (*psychon*) — body DNA-code) shines forth again (Schonberger, 1979).

The *Yijing*, unique in the world of literature and perhaps the oldest book in the world, whose universal significance is, surprisingly, only now becoming clear, was made accessible to the West through the invaluable translation of the German missionary Richard Wilhelm, who even succeeded in rendering these ancient images into comprehensible modern language.

One is not yet justified in reproaching him for being a man of the nineteenth century, informed by the spirit of patriarchal Christianity. Just as with the *Columbus-like* discovery of Freud, Wilhelm's work can be freed of its patriarchal trappings without detracting from its achievement.

Any translation or presentation of the *Yijing* into modern language and idiom will, after removing the patina, always have to orient itself toward Wilhelm's prototype. This is a work of responsibility that Mr. Secter has undertaken with profound effort and success in his *I Ching Clarified*. Even his hexagram names as introductions contain the clarification of many obscure and incomprehensible passages, ideas, and expressions made more obscure by a tradition thousands of years long. This obscurity points to the necessity for such a *guide* for every beginner in this fascinating realm. His book is also valid for praxis gained through long experience with the *Yijing*.

For the purpose of experimental and practical consultation of the *Yijing*, Mr. Secter has found interesting and precise methods that are also convincing to the expert of m any years, such as his original variation of the coin oracle in such a way as to achieve the accuracy of the yarrow stalks method without the expenditure of time.

Also interesting and fruitful is his system that employs a set of unique cards that combine to find and construct the hexagrams. These may be used together with either coins or yarrow stalks. I wish this new and clearer version of the *I Ching* broad circulation for the benefit of mankind.

Dr. Martin Maria Schonberger,
author of *I Ching and the Genetic Code*
—the Hidden Key to Life

This essay was written as the foreword to this book's
German edition, *I Ging Handbuch,* and was rendered
into English from German by Graham Parkes,
Professor of Philosophy, University of Hawaii.

Introduction

There are several ancient cultural traditions that form the pillars that sustain humanity. One of these arose in China and found expression in two figures, Kung Fu Tzu or Kung Ch'iu, better known as Confucius (552–479 B.C.), and Lao Tzu, meaning an old man of wisdom, the father of Daoism, *dao jia*, "school of the way." In actuality, the book known as the *Lao Tzu* is most likely an anthology of writing by more than one teacher.

The social morality of Confucius and the strategical ethic of Lao Tzu both find compatibility in the *I Ching, Book of Change,* whose cosmology, philosophy, and principles have been informing Chinese thinking for will over three thousand years.

What is the I Ching? The question has undoubtedly coexisted with this book since it was first written about 1150 B.C. by King Wen while imprisoned before becoming the first monarch of the Zhou Dynasty. Prior to that time the *1 Ching* was handed down in some form as an oral tradition that credits its beginnings to Fu Xi, the legendary father of Chinese culture.

The *I Ching* is one of the preeminent literary works that have continuously informed Chinese thought. For more than one thousand years it has also informed Korean and Japanese thinking. It addresses such factors as logic, wisdom, ethics, attitudes, interrelatedness, priorities, social values, strategy, harmony, probability, cosmology, investigation, a long view, and a broad perspective.

Behind or within this *I Ching* "system" rests the fundamental concept of assuming full personal responsibility for one's life. At the same time it holds the position that social harmony and cohesion are more important than individual needs or inclinations and that humans are part of a greater natural order and thus subject to common universal principles or processes.

From the time of its earliest recording the *I Ching* seems to have been associated with both philosophy and divination. It owes its profundity to the former, its popularity to the latter, and its exceptional duration to both. For about twenty-five hundred years the *I Ching* has been included among the basic Confucian texts that had to be mastered in the Chinese system of higher education and civil service exams. Passing these formidable exams was like earning a Ph.D. in liberal Arts. Without this degree one could not enter civil service and public administration.

What is so important about the *I Ching?* It represents a way of perceiving the world, particularly human behavior; it indicates a process of thinking about those perceptions; informs a body of mores and ethics that underlie relationships and behavior; and it addresses a perspective on appropriate action. In short it is a guide and a strategy to conscious and ethical living.

Reading or studying the *I Ching* encourages and even compels one to think along its lines, becoming a better person for the experience. Its practicality and wisdom gradually become a resource that resides within one's mind or psyche and serves as a ready source of comfort, support, encouragement, inspiration and reflection.

The *I Ching* has historically attained and maintained a special attraction and interest because of its long, compelling, divinatory reputation. While not denying its divinatory qualities, this has tended to form a misperception in most people's minds. For it is a multifaceted mirror with an inherent potential of reflecting your mind back onto itself, thereby revealing consciousness to itself.

Many people use the *I Ching* to obtain answers to questions. The *I Ching* does not provide answers to anything. It presents the reader with archetypal paradigms, perspectives, and ethics, that serve as models of behavior or ideals to aspire to. With the help of probability, using coins or sticks, it generates a response to an inquiry in the form of a specific hexagram. The ideas within that hexagram are considered relevant but they must be appropriately understood and interpreted for the inquiry.

Beyond the level of the conscious mind, the objective self, logical thinking, deductive reasoning, and an intellectual, analytical approach or response to life's many facets, lies another dimension. Often ignored and unexplored, sometimes experienced, occasionally felt, and too frequently dismissed or maligned, it is the realm of the *metaconscious*.[1] This includes subjective mind and the intuitive, non-concepting "self."

Whereas the conscious spectrum can be understood to be brain-related or "mental," the other realm maybe envisioned as heart-related or "emotional/intuitive." The majority of us are clearly "top-heavy." It would benefit all of us to develop the latter and allow it to move toward fulfilling its potential.

All of us have had the experience at one time or another of doing something intuitively — without a logical or rational reason, perhaps contrary to normal behavior — which changes our life in some meaningful or beneficial way. It may lead us toward an auspicious relationship, into some beneficial experience, or away from difficulty and disaster. When we are cognizant of such occurrences we usually do not pay much attention to them. And when an experience or impression is particularly intense or significant we tend to let it slip by as coincidental. But we know intuition through our experience of it.

You might consider the I *Ching* as a mechanism: to develop intuitive awareness and subjective understanding; as a "key" to exercising or enhancing these abilities; and as a method of accessing or engaging this aspect of oneself or one's self.

The greater the degree to which you exercise and cultivate this quality or to which you stay out of its way and, by not blocking it or interfering with it, allow it to express itself, the more you will be adding a valuable dimension to your life, one that will permit you to experience and relate to the world around and within you more fully. This will enhance your awareness, expand your consciousness, improve your attitude and disposition, and generally enrich the quality of your life.

You may realize or begin to comprehend that what perhaps used to seem as accident, chance, coincidence, fate, or just luck is actually a function of the metaconscious in an intuitive mode, harmonizing or synchronizing with universal or cosmological principles or laws. In China this principal is the *Dao (Tao)*.[2]

It is not necessary to eliminate, negate, avoid, or disregard your intellectual faculties. Rather, by not always depending on or resorting to them, you thereby enable your intuition to blossom and mature. You can gradually learn how to approach and access the intuition, and how to distinguish between clear and obscure impressions. Most important, you develop the ability to act or respond appropriately to intuitive impressions. The original authors of the I *Ching* wisely devised, constructed, and developed this compelling classic to assist in this challenging training and practice. The underlying premise of the I *Ching* is that everything is *tai ji*, "one energy," expressing itself as two opposing but co-creative, mutually interdependent impressions, *yang* and *yin*. This *tai ji* is the sum total of all "existencing." This everything that exists both as being and as potential is in a constant state of flux and transformation. Whereas the yang and yin as a whole are always in balance, they coalesce and interfuse with various ratios of proportion and intensity to harmoniously manifest *dao* or all existencing within *tai ji,* the one universal energy.

The *I Ching* is a microcosm and reflection of this "universal law and order." This, in turn is the "system within which *existencing* is *existencing.*" Each of us exists within the "whole" as a part of it. The *I Ching* helps you become sensitive to the events relative to and relevant to your life. It reveals how to consider or react on the nature, quality, and probable direction of your life within an ethical context.

You learn how, why, and when to act, respond, or refrain from action, so as to be in accord with the dynamic continuum that is within and also *is* this universal, existencing *dao.* This synchronicity will increase the probability of the appropriate and optimal occurring in your life. It will also enhance the probability of the positive — or what you may perceive as positive — materializing and diminish the probability of the negative — or what you perceive as negative — from arising. Your perception of positive and negative, however, may not always be identical to or in agreement with what is actually positive or negative.

As a counsel and advisor the *I Ching* embraces an ethical strategy that represents the optimal, ideal, or most beneficial manner of integrating or harmonizing with the inevitable, for any given condition. This is an ideal. It may be what is best for you or what is best for everyone. And what is best may not appear as such.

For more than twenty-five hundred years the enticement of the *I Ching* has been its reputation as an oracle. Historically it appears to have exhibited a remarkable predisposition toward divination. On the one hand the Chinese people are historically superstitious, while on the other they are a very pragmatic people. It is not easy to reconcile the two. But the *I Ching* seems to have appealed to both Chinese mysticism and practicality. It offers each reader a fascinating approach and process for working toward and achieving a rewarding and fulfilling state of being. The text is the guide, the method or process is the actual significance or meaning, and you are the reason or key to what it is all about.

All existence as existencing is understood in this "system" to be: an aspect of *dao;* in *dao;* in the process of flowing simultaneously toward and from *dao;* in an endless, ever changing disclosure of "being as becoming." Living experience is perceived as "the process of becoming who you are," of consciousness "self-experiencing" or becoming aware of itself.

The *I Ching's* hexagrams essentially represent sixty-four models or aphorisms, short sentences that express a truth or a precept. These are generally called "hexagram texts." While they are easy to read, they are paradoxes and enigmas that are not quickly understood or easily comprehended. This holds true even for the Chinese, whose language is nonlinear and heavily inclined toward inference. All this is in contrast to Western communication, which is generally explicit, straightforward, and anything but vague.

These aphorisms are called *Gua,* a term translated into English as "hexagram" because they are based on six-line figures. Each *Gua* has six sub-aphorisms, one for each of the six lines, called "line texts." Interestingly, when any line text is addressed or read as an addendum to the hexagram text it requires a transformation or change to another specific hexagram.

The mystical writer Rumi, perhaps the most renowned of the Sufi poets, renders an earlier poem that reacts the thinking of the I Ching:

I am your tongue, your eye.
I am your senses, your contentment and anger.
Go, be detached! That one who hears through
me and sees through me is you.
Not only are you the possessor of the secret
but you are the secret too.[3]

It is in this light and with this attitude that the *I Ching* has been read, studied, analyzed, examined, penetrated, used, and counseled with by the greatest scholars and most learned and respected thinkers and leaders of China for more than three thousand years. What is there about the *I Ching* that has merited so much attention and respect for such an extended time?

If you are to benefit from the *I Ching,* it is not necessary to be brilliant, quick, clever, or especially smart. Nor must you be an intellectual, a scholar, an academic, or even a person deeply interested in Chinese history, philosophy, or thought. It is not even required that you approach the *I Ching* seriously or with a profound attitude.

To use this book to advantage you must only be sincere and open. Be receptive to what it has to say, to the process it advocates. You do not even have tobe pre-committed to accepting its advice or following its suggestions. As a friend said:

> *there is a magic in words*
> *that enlighten us to the Truth,*
> *whose meaning constantly expands*
> *to help us to know who we are.*

Thank you for making a place to share this book with you. Wishing you courage in your quest,

—Mondo Secter

PART ONE

DESCRIBING THE I CHING

Outline

This book is intended as a basic introduction and primer to the *I Ching*. At the same time it intends to present something of interest to those readers already familiar or experienced with this Chinese classic. This book follows the conventional approach to what traditionally has been called divination, and what might be better termed *applied predictability*. We might think of it as a treatise on probability, ethics, and strategy, a guide to planning and decision-making.

Within this context, it is important to acknowledge at the outset the potential value of the *I Ching* as an instrument and agency for personal growth. Author Carol Bell Knight said: "Isn't it wonderful how in ancient days, persons of great wisdom wrote words that apply to us today. Use them to infuse your life with who you really are. Use your intuitive, creative imagination to recreate your attitudes, and be at one with the Infinite."[5]

In a very practical way this book can help you learn to tap into yourself, to understand yourself, and to synchronize with the destiny of your own "constantly creating self." You can use this book to take fuller charge of and responsibility for not only your life in general, but also all the choices and decisions you make. In other words, you can learn to experience the nature of your own ego and then learn to cooperate with life.

This can maximize what you can achieve or accomplish, minimize what would burden or diminish you, and optimize your personal integration and fulfillment. Everything and everyone can be enhanced while nobody and nothing is diminished. In this way, you precipitate the best for yourself and others.

You begin with those ordinary activities that consume a substantial portion of daily life. It is possible in addressing these to adventure with the *I Ching* back through the realms of multiplicity, to that part of your *self* that is at one with and in harmony with everything in the universe. In this way you experience that part of "who you are" which is not distinct from everything that exists — the "you" without separation.

This starts as a process of recognition, attunement, and sensitizing that becomes refined as you exercise subjective mind and let it guide you increasingly in your living.

The style of this book will hopefully compel the reader to share fully in the process of constructing an interpretation of the text, and thus assume full responsibility for creative and ethical decision making. At another level the *I Ching* can establish new patterns, models, or paradigms in your mind and consciousness, as well as a framework that can enhance your participation and determination in your life.

Given the vague and implicit nature of the Chinese language, most translations of the *I Ching*, and some interpretations, leave readers confused or mentally struggling with the concepts of the writing, thereby misunderstanding the intent and ideas completely or reading an interpretation into the text that has little to do with its actual meaning.

Many people have commented that there is a subtle Zen-like quality to the manner of this *I Ching* book. While this was not intended there is much from the tradition of *Ch'an* (Zen) that has informed this writer's life. The hexagram and line texts in this book are succinct. They were derived from translations of the original Chinese, primarily those of Richard Wilhelm and, to a lesser extent, John Blofeld.

This *I Ching* book has a writing style that many find to be easy and straightforward. While it is not difficult to read or use, there is nothing simple about it. Its wisdom lies not only in the thoughts and ideas expressed by the original authors,

4

but in the very underlying character of the *I Ching* system itself, as a fully unified cosmology.

It is quite helpful, if not necessary, to gather some basic understanding of how the meanings of the texts and commentaries are derived or constructed. And while this book barely scratches the surface in doing this, what it does cover might make sense and be of value.

Background

Writing this book has taken several years and has been a bold endeavor well beyond this author's level of audacity. It has been a compelling excursion. If this is your first introduction to the *I Ching* or if you have felt alienated or bewildered by other books on the *I Ching*, perhaps this approach will help make the subject and material accessible, interesting, and meaningful. If your interests should increase, then I recommend that you explore books in the list of Suggested Readings.

If you are already familiar with the *I Ching*, this book might add clarification or new insights. And should you be a scholar who has happened upon this book and somehow read this far, you are expressly thanked for bearing with my folly. If there turns out to be but one thing that benefits you or a friend, this book will have served its purpose.

It is not possible to write a book on the *I Ching* without a great deal of introspection and soul-searching. It is somewhat the same if you read or consult with it. Like altering your diet, changes occur to or within you. This has nothing to do with your will or your intent. And it does not matter whether you think you are ready or not. It is the natural outcome of the material and the process fusing with your experiencing in the fourth dimension, time. Any relationship with this non-material, incorporeal, ethical, and guiding energy provokes continual self-examination.

It is inevitable when writing a book such as this to make mistakes and even commit a number of blunders and oversights. Even the contribution of Confucius and his students in writing the *Ten Wings* commentaries on the *I Ching* has been reproached. John Blofeld writes in the introduction to his translation of the *I Ching*: "I base my judgment on what I have read of Confucius' works. It may be that the [*I Ching*] *Commentary on the Text* is not deep enough to do justice to the Text itself."[6] It would seem that one who makes a noble shortcoming in addressing the *I Ching* is at least in good company.

The first translation of note into a Western language was a scholarly work in the late nineteenth century by the Englishman James Legge. A translation by the German missionary Richard Wilhelm was published in 1924. This version was intended to be practical and intelligible to those serious and sincere non-academic readers concerned with their relation to the universe and to their fellow man. It was not until 1950 that Wilhelm's book was published in English. As far as most of us in the West are concerned, this three- thousand-year-old text has been available for less than fifty years.

It did not take long for the profound and enigmatic *I Ching* to capture the attention and imagination of a broad spectrum of people. Its popularity blossomed in the 1960s when many people who became disaffected began to look to the spiritual heritage of the East for meaning, inspiration, and direction. Since then several books on the *I Ching* have appeared, including interpretations, explanations, and translations.

This book introduces new theories and material originated by this author, all of which have been generated from within the *I Ching* system itself. You may find these of interest or value. They are:

1. A new coin method for generating hexagrams that is mathematically compatible with the earlier "yarrow stalk" method

2. This author's hexagram cards, which make it easier to define or form a hexagram as well as understand hexagram structure and the nature of change from one hexagram to another

3. This author's original trigram symbols, which clarify the character and dynamics of the three-lined figures as well as their relationships to each other in forming hexagrams

4. The Transitional Hexagram Theory, that explains the dynamic of intermediate change that occurs when there is more than one Changing Line in a hexagram turning it into another hexagram

5. The Evolutionary Hexagram Theory, that describes each hexagram's primary guiding principle as well as its primary latent distraction or diversion. This is based on the ancient twelve-hexagram "seasonal cycle" that has governed medicine and agriculture in China for over 2000 years (Figure 14, page 63)

The presentation of this book adopts a minimalist approach, at least insofar as the traditional commentaries are concerned. At the same time the commentaries are comfortably colloquial. So whereas the hexagram images, ideas, and impressions may initially be elusive, the language is easy to understand.

Each hexagram text is reduced to the simplest and shortest form possible while still retaining its essential idea, character, integrity, and grace. This approach encourages, allows, requires, and even demands that you, the reader, exert a creative, intuitive, and subjective effort to fill in the spaces and complete the picture of your own understanding. This is both a challenge and an opportunity.

What is the *I Ching*?

A few words can not responsibly explain even in a small way what the *I Ching* is. That would require several volumes. And while extensive reading will give you much information about the *I Ching*, it will not give you any real understanding. It is fundamentally an interactive, experiential, and potentially transformational phenomenon. In fact translating the *I Ching* as "Book of Change" does not represent the kind of change expressed. This is nothing short of transformational change. A title in English could appropriately be "Book of Transformation."

The *I Ching* is one of the world's oldest, continuously read, living, spiritual, ethical, and philosophical texts — and perhaps the most enigmatic. Its origins are traced back to a legendary person named Fu Xi, who according to tradition lived about five thousand years ago. The father of much of Chinese culture, Fu Xi is credited with originating the yin – yang system and the *ba gua* or eight figures, better known as trigrams.

The sixty-four hexagram texts and the sequential order as it is known today were first recorded around 1150 B.C. by King Wen, founder of the Zhou Dynasty. A short time later his son wrote the six "line texts" that are appended to each hexagram. It was about six hundred years later, that Confucius, or more probably his senior students and followers, added the *Ten Wings*, a comprehensive body of commentaries based on the master's teachings. These writings provide valuable understanding and insight into the *I Ching*.

The philosophical and ethical content of the *I Ching*, both inherent and expressed, are integral to Daoism, Confucianism, and *Ch'an* (Zen) Buddhism. With three thousand years of divinatory popularity and philosophical prominence, its influence on Oriental thought and culture has been all-encompassing and nothing short of remarkable. Its impact can be noted today informing the spiritual, religious, and social values of more than one quarter of the world's people.

The *I Ching* has always been held in the highest esteem by the most respected and renowned leaders, philosophers, emperors, educators, and officials of China. It was not only what we call "required reading" for the civil service exams but also as part of the Confucian classics, it formed the basis for all education in China for twenty-five hundred years. In addition, it was considered one of the primary references in every family and public library.

Its reputation as an oracle of divination significantly predates its recorded history. When used correctly, the *I Ching* provides enlightening comments on one's perception or point of view of a particular circumstance in the past, present, or future. It includes suggestions on how best to address or deal with these conditions.

In addition, the *I Ching* provides an awareness of insight, a sense of ethical priority, a holistic perspective, and an assuring grounding, frame of reference, and sense of direction to those seeking its guidance or counsel. Should you approach the *I Ching* in a proper and sincere manner, with a question or inquiry, you can expect an appropriate and meaningful response. In other words, you allow an answer or a solution to introduce or present itself. It then remains up to you to learn how to interpret and apply the ideas as they pertain to a particular situation. This is accomplished through practice, perseverance, experience, and introspection.

This approach may be compared to the Zen artist who carves "mindlessly" on a block of wood to disclose the sculpture always there waiting to be revealed. These same sentiments are expressed in the writing of the great artist Michelangelo, who in spite of his immense talent and creative genius was continually amazed at the profound beauty his chisel exposed in the marble.[7]

Consider the *I Ching* also as a "universing" model or paradigm that expresses the mutually informing, inter-connective co-creating of which everything is an expression and apart from which there is no existing. This idea is informed and expressed through the very system of the *I Ching*, which is a three thousand year old Chinese classical text of semiotic significance and importance. The *I Ching* conveys more through what it is than through what it says. This is something to be discovered.

Regardless of how you think of using the *I Ching*, whether for divination, inspiration, reflection, or philosophical insight, it is best to treat its words as those of a wise companion, benevolent stranger, or impartial friend whose considerations and thoughts can provide you with a deeper understanding of life's conditions and your personal potential, spiritual and temporal.

The Composition of the *I Ching*

The body of the *I Ching* is based on sixty-four *gua*, six-lined binary configurations, usually called hexagrams. Each of these is accompanied by a brief text that portrays the meaning or idea of the hexagram. In addition, there are short texts, one for each of the six lines. These indicate the significance of that line in relation to the other five, and also the specific influences, notions, ideas, or meanings that are lost or gained when that line becomes changed into its opposite; yang to yin or yin to yang.

The traditional manner of using or engaging the *I Ching* is to formulate an inquiry in the prescribed manner, respectfully and sincerely. The process is described in detail in Wilhelm's *I Ching* book. You then manipulate fifty sticks or toss three coins in a procedure that is repeated six times. This will define or construct a particular hexagram that serves as the opinion, advice, or counsel for the original inquiry. In many instances you will also be directed to refer to or read an additional line text.

Where one or more of the line texts is indicated, you are further required to read the text for another specific hexagram. This reveals a probable change in condition from what is described by the first hexagram to what is described by the second. Where no change is indicated, the hexagram is considered essentially static, at least for the time being. This means that the condition described by the initial hexagram completely governs the response to your inquiry.

Static responses are generally less complicated to interpret. A response involving one or more changes to other hexagrams is more involved and time consuming. This book adopts an approach that reduces or eliminates most of the linguistic dilemmas, confusing references, puzzling implications, and remote cultural concepts inherent in the original Chinese.

Your initial interest in the *I Ching* may primarily be in its divination, its oracular capacity, or even its philosophical and ethical impressions. Nevertheless it is helpful to remember that this text can function at the same time to reinform your mind in such a way as to enhance your awareness, perception, and insight. This sensitizing is an unfolding that takes place gradually over a period of time, although it is not unusual for one to experience it apparently suddenly or become suddenly aware of it.

It is probable that with diligence, self-reflection, and introspection you will subtly repattern the manner in which you perceive, analyze, organize, respond to, and interact with those impressions that constitute your reality. Slowly and by degree, you will become aware of the changes within you. This is not something to strive for, but rather to understand as a beneficial eventuality when it is realized — a positive by-product of the manner in which you are engaging your life. Personal growth and insight are realized in their own sweet time.

How Does the *I Ching* Work?

As an oracle or method of divination, the *I Ching* operates in such a way as to demonstrate or reflect the connection or relationship you have with the *dao*, that "eternal now" from which you are never separated. This occurs in a manner that metaphorically freezes the present moment at the time of casting a hexagram in response to your inquiry, even while the present continues to unfold. An inquiry about the future addresses a future that for now exists only in your present mind. As a projection and probability this future is essentially a function of your present minding.

The *I Ching* somehow allows you to make a mental image of a present mind-moment relative to your inquiry, a photograph-like mind-impression of a thought-reflection that you can observe and reflect on, and then act on accordingly. Consider an analogy:

You are driving a car and pass over a transparent bridge. From below, a photograph or video is taken of the car and projected onto a small screen by the radio. While you continue driving on the road, you look at the picture and notice that one of the tires is bald, another has a nail in the side of it, and there is evidence of an oil leak. You have not yet experienced any problems. What you decide is up to you.

In this example the camera represents your metaconscious. The photograph, like the *I Ching*, portrays your mind on which the information or data is presented or reflected.

When you are casting a hexagram (see page 43), you connect or align your conscious to the metaconscious, uniting your subjective, intuitive mind with your objective, intellectual mind. This establishes a mechanism by which you consciously grasp a metaconscious awareness relative to your particular inquiry, whether the inquiry is expressed or not. The freer your conscious or unconscious mind is from distractions, preoccupations, or obscurations, the more it will be in alignment with the metaconscious, and therefore the clearer and more relevant you can expect the response and your perception of the response to be.

Where you have not completely cleared your mind with a few moments of meditation or calm, if you ask a question but have another matter or concern preoccupying your mind, or if you are otherwise distracted by extraneous thoughts or unrelated concerns, you will likely receive a muddled, confusing, or misplaced response. In such cases the hexagram you receive may not be a response to your inquiry. Rather it could be a response to the unstated concern that is subconsciously interfering with or distracting you. This may be a message you need to hear or consider. But you should recognize that the response addresses your unstated concern and not your written or intended inquiry.

In Chinese, the same character is used for both *heart* and *mind*. The Buddhist term for intuitive mind is "inner heart." By allowing your "inner heart" to settle on a particular inquiry, while simultaneously separating or withdrawing your deliberate or conscious perceptions from extraneous or irrelevant thoughts as much as possible, the metaconscious has the opportunity to disclose itself or activate on your behalf. This is precipitated by means of the casting method.

I Ching as Practice

You may read or hear that one should not use the *I Ching* except for serious or important questions or concerns. This is not necessarily so. In response to this position it may be said that serious questions and concerns should be addressed sincerely. The *I Ching* is not a mechanical device or electrical appliance that you turn off and on as a matter of convenience.

One comes to learn and understand the *I Ching* by regular use and practice until one is familiar and comfortable with it, until one has incorporated it as a system or cosmology within oneself, until it is like playing a musical instrument, and until it becomes an extension of yourself. It is not something straightforward and technical. Rather it is something you have to learn and come to terms with. The *I Ching* is not something you can master, but something that you will be humbled by.

The best recommendation is to begin by using the *I Ching* regularly and informally in order to become knowledgeable in its ways, familiar with its character, and comfortable with its manner of communicating. More importantly it should be used to enhance sensitivity of and toward yourself. This constitutes an exercise and practice in attunement. It is a process that unfolds through application of effort, inner attention, focus, and correct intent. The *I Ching* is a subtle, profound, and enigmatic work that embraces and inter-weaves elements of philosophy, psychology, management, administration, and strategy to name a few. It is a semiotic system in which symbols represent ideas, ideas represent words, and words represent other symbols or even words other than themselves.

Trigrams Explained

The next few pages outline the basic elements of forming an inquiry and casting a hexagram in response to that inquiry. It is presented here to provide you with a helpful framework within which to better grasp the material in the following chapters.

1. Write down your inquiry, being brief and specific. Avoid ambiguity, even in dealing with a general condition. Do not ask questions that can be answered with a "yes" or "no." It is also best to indicate a time frame within which the inquiry is constructed or phrased, for example six days, three weeks, or five months.

2. With the inquiry in mind, take a minute or so to become calm, relaxed, and as centered as possible. One way to do this is to close your eyes and allow your breathing to slow down.

3. The coin method casting procedure is explained on page 44. The stick method is described on page 48. You will repeat the process six times, once for each line of the hexagram.

4. Each casting will generate one of four numerical values: 6, 7, 8, or 9. The symbols for these are: 6 —x— ; 7 ———; 8 — — ; 9 —o— . Lines with a value of 6 or 9 are called Changing Lines or Moving Lines (see Changing Lines, page 53).

5. If the first line is 7, you draw ———. If the second line is 9, you draw —o— above the ———: ═o═ . If the third line is 8, you draw — — above the ═o═ : ═o═ . No 6 —x— or 9 —o— lines means the hexagram is stable and does not undergo change.

6. These first three lines are called the Lower Trigram. They form the bottom half or inner structure of the hexagram.

7. Repeat the casting three more times for a total of six lines. Consider, for example, that they are 6 —x— , 8 — —, 7 ———. These three lines ═══ are the Upper Trigram which forms the top half or external structure of the hexagram.

8. The lower trigram and upper trigram combine to form a hexagram. To determine the hexagram number you can either use the *I Ching* hexagram cards included with this book (see page 158), or refer to the chart on page 162.

9. Note that using either cards or the chart there are two numbers. The large number represents the Basic Hexagram while the smaller number represents the Evolutionary Hexagram, (see page 61). In this example, the two trigrams form Hexagram 41 with two changing lines: ═══

10. The following steps relate to reading and interpreting the response. You first turn to the Commentaries in Part Two and read the text for Hexagram 41 (page 138). This consists of the first paragraph only which outlines the hexagram perspective.

11. Next you will read the line text for the first (lowest) changing line. In this example it is line 2, —o— . The line text either modifies, augments, or supersedes the Basic Hexagram text depending on the particular hexagram.

12. At the end of the line text is a number. This indicates the Changed Hexagram; that is, the hexagram that transpires or that this Basic Hexagram transforms into as a result of the first changing line. In this example, Hexagram 41 changes to Hexagram 27. Therefore you read the first paragraph which constitutes Hexagram 27's basic text. This describes the changed condition that arises necessarily and unavoidably.

13. If there were only one changing line, the reading for the casting would stop there. In this example however there is a second changing line at line 4, —x— . You therefore read the text for Hexagram 27, line 4. The information in this text will either modify, augment, or supersede this Basic Hexagram text.

14. At the end of the text for Hexagram 27, line 4, there is the number 21. This is the number of the Changed Hexagram. As there are no additional changing lines the Changed Hexagram is also the Ending Hexagram.

15. The Ending Hexagram expresses that significant condition or state to which the Basic Hexagram develops or resolves itself within the stated or implied time frame. Remember that nothing is fixed or concrete, so whether you like or dislike the response it is only a transitory state with regard to the inquiry.

16. Where time is a factor or condition the positions of the lines usually reflect relative time. The closer to the bottom or beginning of a hexagram a Changing Line occurs or is situated, the sooner its conditions will take effect. Conversely, the closer a Changing Line is to the top or end of a hexagram, the later its conditions will take effect.

The subsequent chapters explain additional steps and some subtle factors to take into consideration when interpreting a response to an inquiry. Remember, this introductory explanation is just a brief overview or preview to help put the following information into a meaningful context. You might reread this section once or twice before proceeding so as to be comfortable with the general process of using the *I Ching* to cast a hexagram. (See the chapters on Casting and Changing Lines for more information on Time and Change in the *I Ching*.)

Trigram Development — Yang and Yin

The philosophy and experience of the *I Ching* begins with *tai ji*, the Supreme Ultimate, that Unmanifest Essence which is the universe itself. When it does manifest it expresses itself as two inseparable, complementary, coexisting energies: yang ——— and yin — — . The symbol for yang is an undivided line: solid, closed, unyielding, and impenetrable; The symbol for yin is a divided line: diffuse, open, yielding, and responsive.

In general terms, yang discloses itself as active, firm, light, initiative, contractive, immaterial, affirming, turned on, sustaining, and positive.

Yin discloses itself as passive, dark, material, yielding, soft expansive, nourishing, pliable, turned off, and negative.

All objects, situations, perceptions, and concepts are composed of the interblending of yang and yin in varying proportions. Except theoretically there is nothing that is totally or exclusively yin or yang. Theoretically the yang line represents those qualities that are purely yang, and the yin line reflects those qualities that are purely yin. In actuality the most extreme or absolute yang has some yin, and the most extreme or absolute yin has some yang.

The second layer of differentiation expands to include two lines. This represents an expanded or refined clarification of relative *yang-ness* and *yin-ness*. The four two-lined figures listed below with explanations reveal their primary characteristics.

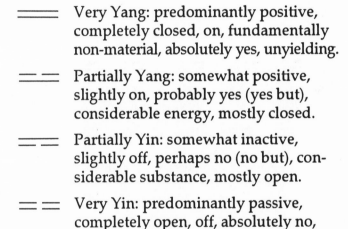

Very Yang: predominantly positive, completely closed, on, fundamentally non-material, absolutely yes, unyielding.

Partially Yang: somewhat positive, slightly on, probably yes (yes but), considerable energy, mostly closed.

Partially Yin: somewhat inactive, slightly off, perhaps no (no but), considerable substance, mostly open.

Very Yin: predominantly passive, completely open, off, absolutely no, fundamentally material, yielding.

When a third line is added to the four two-line combinations above they form or yield the eight trigrams (or *gua*, with a small "g"). *Gua* may be translated as *configuration* or *diagram*, and in the *I Ching* means either trigram or hexagram. Where the word *gua* is used for hexagram it will have a capital "G," as in *Gua*. When two *gua* are joined together, one above the other, a hexagram is formed. There are a total of 8 x 8 or sixty-four hexagrams (p. 162).

7	6	5	4	3	2	1	0
QIAN	DUI	LI	JEN	SUN	KAN	GEN	KUN
Heaven	Ocean	Flame	Thunder	Wind	River	Mountain	Earth

Figure 2. Evolution of the Eight Trigrams

THE EIGHT TRIGRAMS

In the *I Ching*, each of the trigrams expresses one of the eight categories or aspects of *tai ji*, Universal Substance. Each of these represents an aggregate of distance, expressive, dynamic, complex, phenomena or energies. In order to grasp the meanings inherent in each *gua* and to facilitate understanding the composite of ideas they embody, they became associated with or related to familiar concepts, which in turn represented categories of experience.

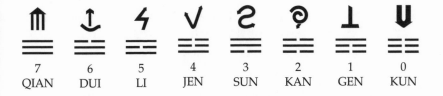

7	6	5	4	3	2	1	0
QIAN	DUI	LI	JEN	SUN	KAN	GEN	KUN

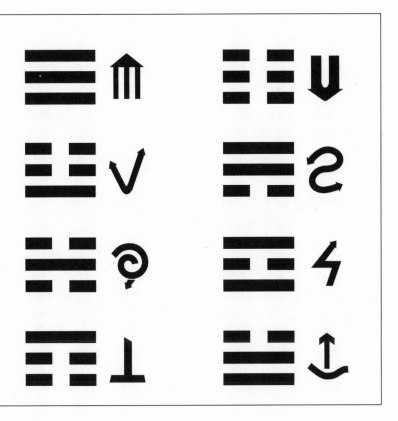

Figure 3. New Trigram Symbols

The following is a partial list which indicates the main conceptual categories by or through which you can begin to comprehend the properties of eight *gua*. Each *gua* is related to:

1. one of the eight members of the archetypal family, denoting qualities, not gender

2. an element or category of the natural order

3. personality characteristics and disposition

4. a part of the body and related attitudes, functions, and implications

5. a product or element in nature and an animal form representing an innate behavior type

6. a color vibration and a compass setting indicating geographic and climatic types

7. body type and social/sexual temperament, inclination, or disposition

8. a season of the year and a time period of the day

The qualities and characteristics of the sixty-four *Gua* or hexagrams are to a large extent then derived from or expressed through the dynamic relationship existing as a function of the two component trigrams. To reasonably understand the manner in which any two trigrams interact requires a thorough comprehension of the trigrams. Some of this is acquired intellectually but most of it comes about through direct experience with the *I Ching* which enhances intuitive understanding.

To assist in furthering your understanding of the trigrams, this author has devised a set of eight graphic symbols, one for each of the eight *gua*. These were designed or derived from ideas inherent in the original text as well as information expressed in the *Ten Wings, Confucian Commentaries*.

The intention is not to replace the *gua* but to support them with meaningful symbols, helpful to the reader. There is no single diagram that could adequately represent the complexity of each *gua* apart from the traditional three-line *gua* symbols themselves. Many people, however, have found using the *gua* and the symbols together uniquely beneficial, especially in grasping the inner dynamics of the hexagrams.

An arrow within the symbol indicates the primary direction or quality of motion. The form or design of the line indicates the nature or spirit of that motion. These symbols are used throughout this book alongside the trigrams of each hexagram. Hopefully they convey the nature and direction of trigram energy and motion in a way that facilitates or furthers understanding of the hexagrams.

The figure on page 32 is a diagram of the circular arrangement of the trigrams with each symbol occupying its respective position on the compass. This is credited to King Wen, author of the *I Ching*. The Chinese traditionally place "south" on the top and "north" on the bottom, with "east" and "west" in the familiar place. This diagram has "north" at the top. The inside portion of the circle represents the bottom of each symbol and the outside is the top of the symbol.

The Character of the Eight Trigrams

QIAN / Chien

1. father, principled, serious, authoritarian, defending
2. heaven, space, pure energy, without material substance
3. resolute, unswerving, positive, inflexible, unyielding, firm
4. the head: initiative, strength, dominant, affirmation, stern
5. metal, hard and cold; a lean horse, efficient, compact
6. deep red, purple, burgundy; northwest
7. solid, muscular, masculine, aggressive; potent, virile, lusty
8. early winter and late evening until 11:00 p.m.

QIAN moves straight, upward, or forward, as an advancing force that ultimately can penetrate and push through or apart anything in its way. When in motion it has the power of a rocket; at rest the stability of a tripod. Its columns support a roof or cover that will house, shade, or protect whatever comes under its mantle or within its boundaries or sphere of influence.

This is the field of universal energy and spiritual, ethical mind force. Its qualities encompass resolution, judgment, power and will. These are tempered by experience, purity of intention, stature, and endurance. *Qian* is tireless, fearless, dispassionate, unemotional, and impassive with no time to waste. It symbolizes oneness, determination, majesty, and high principles.

KUN / Kun

1. mother, venerable, worldly wise, humanitarian
2. earth, substance, material, mineral, matter
3. expansive, yielding, negation, adaptable, harmonious, frugal
4. the belly: sheltering, resilient, safeguard, enclose, receive
5. soil, soft and accepting; (pregnant) cow, gentle, abundant
6. pitch black, total darkness, all absorbing; southwest
7. ample, loving, generous, fleshy; amorous, affectionate
8. early autumn afternoon or very late night 1:30–4:00

KUN's movement is not initiating but receiving, sinking down into and with its mass. It is not a single entity but a cohesive collection of individual particulars, an assembled multiplicity. *Kun* is the manifestation of essence, that which is material and dynamically at rest, completely free of tension or pressure. It is fundamentally open and nourishing, without a personal agenda.

This expresses the perfection of fulfillment, the embodiment of all that is substantive or has material form. It represents fertility, reproduction, birthing, selflessness, impartiality, and continuation. As such it is gentle, nourishing, maternal, loving, and sheltering. *Kun* is spread out, and while it has no particular form it symbolizes all form and that which ripens and matures.

JEN / Ren

1. eldest son, energetic, speculative, adventurous
2. thunder, sound waves, echo, communication, ricochet, rebound
3. arousing, instigating, stimulating, energizing, impulsive
4. the feet: action, enterprising, resourceful, mercuric, swift, dashing
5. grain, bamboo, agile, resilient, skillful; a dragon
6. deep yellow, ocher, flaxen, orange; east
7. lean, wiry, athletic; arousing, imaginative, versatile
8. spring and early morning

JEN has such speed it seems to be in two places at once or moving in two directions at the same time. It rebounds and ricochets quickly traveling in straight lines that form an interior angle that serves as a resonating chamber. This can project sound far or wide depending on its configuration. *Jen* is vibrant, stimulating, and blessed with resiliency and versatility.

This *gua* represents beginning, emergence and manifestation. Of the eight trigrams it is the most swift and expeditious. Universally oriented and always on the go, it has vigor, vitality and a decisiveness and enthusiasm that impels, propels, compels, and stimulates others to action. *Jen* is always planting seeds and ideas as it blends material and spiritual in an unceasing quest.

SUN / Sun

1. eldest daughter, self-assured, purposeful, determined
2. wind, plants, pliable, supple, penetrating, dispersing
3. gentle, adaptable, elusive, insinuating, suggestive
4. the thighs: subtle, cognizant, vigorous, encompassing
5. trees, plants, flexible, elastic; a rooster, familiar, proud
6. white, silver, reflective; southeast
7. voluptuous, shapely, endowed; amorous, alluring, erogenous
8. early summer and mid-morning

SUN moves around curvaceously, sometimes quickly, sometimes slowly, with the ability to proceed in many directions at the same time, and the capacity to simultaneously envelope and penetrate, often in ways that are comfortable and caressing. Its seductive character may not become apparent until it is too late.

There is a quality about this *gua* that hovers on the edge of precarious, usually managing to retain its delicate balance and impunity. Constantly advancing and retreating, it is the most cerebral, unpredictable, and changeable energy. *Sun* is intense, proud, self-assured, resilient, and inviting. It is sensual, active and mature, permeating and yielding at the same time.

KAN / G'an

1. middle son, wild, courageous, melancholy, abysmal
2. rivers, rain, sleet, snow, canyons, rift, contend, challenge
3. frustrated, misleading, deceptive, prejudiced, insecure
4. the ears: attentive, musical, emotional, distraught, confused, rugged
5. dry wood, timber, logs, rigid; wild pig or boar, fearless
6. bright red; north
7. portly, chubby, corpulent; lascivious, erotic, provocative
8. winter and midnight

KAN is that which is always falling, tumbling, flowing, streaming, and swirling unpredictably down and around. It depicts rain, snow, sleet, hail, and storms as well as water flowing on and under the ground toward its destination. *Kan* also connotes water's erosion in the form of canyons, abysses, caverns, and dry river beds. It is almost always circuitous, contained, and confined.

In the same way that rivers are contained within their banks this *gua* expresses confinement of a "heart and soul" locked within the body; unfulfilled yearning; heartache and melancholy. *Kan* plunges into things, is usually diligent and rarely shirks responsibility But constant frustration can easily lead it to changing course or using questionable or deceptive means to achieve its ends.

LI / Li

1. middle daughter, dependent, devotion, indecisive
2. sun, flame, light, laser, warmth, attachment, clinging
3. temperamental, hot, explosive, clever, spicy, sarcastic
4. the eyes: perceptive, visual, quick, sharp, inconsistent
5. fire, combustion; pheasant, exquisite bird
6. yellow, blazing; south
7. lithe, gorgeous, dazzling; passionate, igniting
8. summer and noontime

LI proceeds slowly forward and upward occasionally with sudden and incredible bursts of energy. When not proceeding directly ahead it may pause or move laterally in what appears to be an erratic, indecisive, or evasive manner. *Li* rarely returns or retreats. Although totally dependent, it tends to consume almost everything in its path, a course that can be self-destructive.

This *gua* symbolizes clarity of consciousness and psychic or intuitive awareness. There is something mysterious to this entity. It is emotionally and intellectually quick and yet, physically it is usually but not always slow moving. *Li* is sociable, bright, communicative, and impassioned, arousing those on whom it depends. Resistant on the outside, it tends to be dry, empty, and yielding within.

GEN / Ken

1. youngest son, protective, steadfast, stalwart
2. mountain, massive, keeping still, solid, sturdy, committed
3. responsible, introspective, dependable, reliable, faithful
4. the hands: reassuring, humility, reserved, helpful
5. solid rock, stone, coniferous; dog, canine
6. green, luscious; northeast
7. stocky, strong; endurance, stamina, pragmatic
8. early spring and daybreak, sunrise or pre-dawn

GEN pushes upward and presses downward simultaneously, but is basically immobile and still. Any movement could disrupt everything around, and a significant shift would be devastating. As a rule, *Gen* can withstand any confrontation and is therefore given a wide berth or encountered congenially. Introspective and self-assured, it exerts stability and exceptional will power.

This *gua* embodies the mystery of metaphysical beginning and ending, meaning it addresses the questions of expansion and motion; of space and time. It is essentially grounded, immovable, remote, resisting, and indestructible, and as such is associated with reliability, faithfulness, guarding and defending others. Symbolic of action at rest, *Gen* is the gateway to inner spirit.

DUI

1. youngest daughter, joyful, mischievous, deleterious,
2. lake, marsh, ocean, casual, easy going, manipulative
3. playful, irresponsible, innocence, precocious, immature
4. the mouth, flesh: sensual, attracting, inviting, playful, provocative
5. pond; sheep or goat, ruinous, dangerous, destructive
6. blue; west
7. nubile, ripe; tempting, beguiling, flirtatious, exciting
8. autumn and late afternoon or early evening

DUI undulates like the water of a lake or ocean. Its surface usually ripples playfully, but occasionally is threatening and intense. Above, it appears basically calm and stable, but deeper within or below lies mystery, dangers, and extreme pressure. This is in contrast to the excitement, pleasure, and relative security above. While settling downward, *Dui* evaporates subtly upward.

This *gua* expresses the mysterious ocean depths that resist being thoroughly explored or known. Its attractions are enticing, but they also harbor unanticipated, unknown and lurking dangers. *Dui* can warm and delight the cold-hearted and can break up or destroy the unwary and negligent. It is gregarious and colorful, and may be enjoyed but with prudence and caution.

The diagram below shows each trigram according to its position on the compass, its related season of the year, and its approximate time of day.

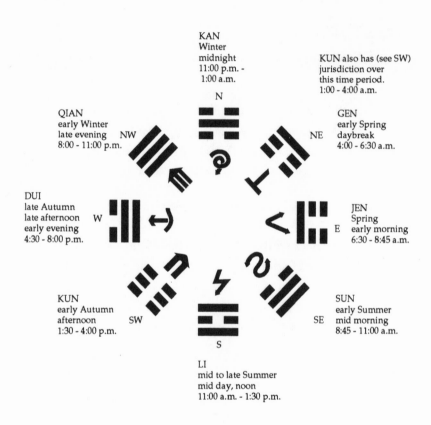

KAN
Winter
midnight
11:00 p.m. -
1:00 a.m.

N

KUN also has (see SW)
jurisdiction over
this time period.
1:00 - 4:00 a.m.

QIAN
early Winter
late evening   NW
8:00 - 11:00 p.m.

GEN
early Spring
NE   daybreak
4:00 - 6:30 a.m.

DUI
late Autumn
late afternoon   W
early evening
4:30 - 8:00 p.m.

JEN
Spring
E   early morning
6:30 - 8:45 a.m.

KUN
early Autumn
afternoon   SW
1:30 - 4:00 p.m.

SUN
early Summer
SE   mid morning
8:45 - 11:00 a.m.

S

LI
mid to late Summer
mid day, noon
11:00 a.m. - 1:30 p.m.

Figure 4. Circular Arrangement of the Eight Trigrams
According to King Wen, 1150 B.C.

32

FORMING AND COMPREHENDING HEXAGRAMS

A *Gua* or hexagram is formed when two *gua* or trigrams are configured, one over the other. Trigrams, as already explained, are constructed of three lines that are yang (undivided) ——, or yin (divided) — — and stacked one above the other. Whether a line is undivided or divided is determined by methods of apparent chance or probability, of which two are described in the section on "Casting the *I Ching*."

Hexagrams are semiotic. They are symbols that convey ideas, words, and other symbols or sets of symbolic relationships. In the *I Ching*, each individual hexagram contains a complex set of overlapping, interacting, and intermingled images. These in turn are represented by a Chinese character or *ideogram* that contains an additional set of concepts which can not be easily defined or translated by a few words. The explication of hexagrams is the result of the following sets of ideas.

Trigram Relationships

This refers to the dynamic which is established, expressed, or set in motion between the lower and upper trigrams. You will learn to comprehend how the two *gua* are mutually reinforcing or antagonistic, advancing or obstructing, supportive or inhibiting, friendly or hostile. You will easily recognize harmony, friction, compatibility, and conflict. This will be made more lucid with the aid of the symbols when they are used together with the trigrams.

These symbols not only depict the movement, action, and energy within each trigram, but also more importantly, between the trigrams. You will acquire an intuitive sense of this. Whenever you depict a hexagram on paper, you might draw your own version of the symbols to the right of the two component trigrams similar to the manner used throughout this book.

When two trigrams are moving in the same or a similar direction, they tend to support or reinforce each other. When they are moving in opposite directions, they tend to block, inhibit, or pull apart from each other. When they are moving in other ways, they might distract, aggravate, or frustrate one another. There are possible exceptions as when two paired trigrams are of similar maturity: mother and father; eldest sister and eldest brother; etc. It will take experience and practice to learn this intuitively. Even then there are dimensions of trigram character that seem to remain elusive.

Hexagram Image

This deals with comprehending or perceiving the hexagrams as complete images in which the lines are in a state of interaction or relative balance with each other. The concept is not difficult once you understand the idea and the methodology. The undivided yang lines and the divided yin lines are understood as dynamic entities or energies in which the lines are collectively moving upward or forward as the case may be, like passengers on a train, plane, or ship.

Within this image, the yang lines represent consolidated, unified energy, actively and powerfully driving upward or forward, whereas the yin lines represent collective, cooperative energy energetically but passively pressing downward. Imagine a large crowd pushing in one direction while you are going the opposite way. When there is one or more yin line immediately above or in front of a yang line, that yang line is theoretically facing little or no resistance or obstruction. When however a yang line has one or more yin lines on either side of it, it could be theoretically hemmed in. Hexagram lines may also be viewed as forms of relative balance or imbalance. These are learned through experience and not intellectually.

For example in Hexagram 28 whose name may be expressed as Excessive, Overburdened, and Overextended, we see four yang lines in the middle flanked by two yin lines, one each at the top and bottom: ☰☰ The Commentary of the *I Ching* compares this to the roof beam of a house that is heavy and strong in the middle area but thin and weak at the two ends. Inadequately supported, the beam is about to collapse. This hexagram is the model for every condition that has a poor or inadequate support system.

A second example is Hexagram 46 whose name is Striving, Ambitious, and Orchestrated. The second and third lines are yang while the other four are yin: ☰☰ The Commentary indicates that the yang lines are already set in motion with nothing blocking the way. The two yang lines reinforce each other in moving upward. Their position indicates the motion has already begun.

A third example here is Hexagram 20, titled Composure, Awareness, and Contemplation. The bottom four lines are yin while the top two are yang: ☰☰ We are informed that this is in effect a doubling of the trigram *gen* ☰☰, or a model of *gen* intensified (see page 30).

Hexagram Lines as a Field of Energy

Whereas the aforementioned explanation of Hexagram Image describes an interaction between yang and yin lines within a *Gua*, this explanation profiles the interaction between a force encountering, entering, and transiting a field of lines or energy from the bottom. That is, the hexagram is viewed as a territory you must negotiate, in which the lines are entities that on one hand can distract or obstruct you or on the other support your effort.

Depending on various factors, the yang lines may block you, or if you can synchronize with them, either slipstream in their wake, get a boost, or catch a ride. When the bottom line is divided, there is generally no initial obstruction. But unless all the lines are divided as in Hexagram 2 ☰☰

you can expect to meet up with one sooner or later. If the bottom line is undivided you have to look further to know how to approach the hexagram. It might help to take a brief look at the same three hexagrams used in the previous examples but from a different viewpoint.

One who must deal with Hexagram 28, Excessive, Over-burdened, and Overextended ☰ should realize that the slightest thing could precipitate complete break down or collapse. While easy to enter, a massive barrier of four yang lines is quickly confronted. One might successfully negotiate the first of these but there is no way to effectively manage or traverse all four. In addition they represent a formidable energy which resists all attempts to alter its course. When #28 is encountered use strength and caution to steer a safe course until an alternative presents itself.

In the case of Hexagram 46, Striving, Ambitious, and Orchestrated ☱ , there are only two yang lines following the initial yin line. If one enters with confidence and enthusiasm, it is possible to give those two lines the boost they need to get to the top. The more energy that is expended at the start, the faster the subsequent action or reaction. It helps to have a clear and well thought out plan to avoid hastening astray.

In the preceding section's example of Hexagram 20, Composure, Awareness, and Contemplation ☲ , the way is apparently unobstructed. Since it is difficult to clearly see more than two or three lines ahead, the two yang lines are probably not perceived until one is already committed and into the hexagram. One who starts too fast will undoubtedly collide in surprise or frustration near the end. An open path usually is a signal to proceed confidently but with care.

It would require a separate volume to consider each hexagram thoroughly. The intent is to facilitate your awareness of the essential symbolic constituents which broaden the understanding of hexagram meaning.

Hexagram 5: PAUSING, Biding Time, Deliberate Waiting

This *Gua* is composed of the lower trigram *qian* and the upper trigram *kan*. *Qian*, as father, unswerving power, and pure energy forging upward, encounters *kan*, as middle son, contentious, and emotional, spiraling downward like a whirlpool. This presents *qian* with a difficult, dangerous, time-consuming confrontation. Whereas the all-powerful should eventually penetrate any obstruction of this kind, there could be minor damage or abrasions and unnecessary delay. The wise choice is to pause briefly and review the conditions, as well as the available options on how best to negotiate the situation. Take time to observe *kan*'s behavior and give it time to dissipate.

Hexagram 36: CONSTRAINT, Suppression, Tyranny

In this *Gua* are the lower trigram *li* and the upper trigram *kun*. *Li*, middle daughter, light, flame, vision, and clarity is shining upward but it is suppressed or smothered by *kun*, mother, darkness, earth which settles downward absorbing all of *li*'s light. The younger *li* is weaker and less experienced and unable to penetrate this thick blanket of darkness. Under these circumstances it becomes advisable not to reflect or shine your light but to keep it concealed for the present time. This not only saves energy but also avoids tempting those who would like to possess, exploit, injure, or misuse your bright assets.

Hexagram 61: INSTINCTIVE, Authentic, Innate

This *Gua* is formed by the lower trigram *dui* and the upper trigram *sun*. *Dui*, the youngest daughter is playful, carefree, and potentially troublesome, whereas *sun*, the eldest daughter is elusive, insinuating, experienced, and responsible. When wind blows over the water slowly, it calms the surface. But when it blows strongly, it agitates the waves dangerously. The name of this *Gua* is not based on the dynamic interaction between the trigrams, but is derived from the total image of the lines. The hexagram's six lines represent a doubling or an intensification of the three lines in the trigram *li*. This indicates a deepening of the essential quality of *li*, namely sight and vision. It is that which allows people to know or see others for who they are and allows you to see things for what they really are.

Line Relationships

This is one of the more difficult components to interpreting the *I Ching*. Even after understanding its concepts intellectually there remains something elusive about the real meanings underlying the ideas expressed by the line relationships.

Each of the six lines has its own attributes and functions, its individual relationships to the other lines, and its place with regard to the hexagram as a whole. This becomes especially important with Changing Lines because there is a fundamental shift in the dynamics. Having a grasp of "line mechanics" helps to focus on an aspect of interpretation that may be specifically relevant to your inquiry (see page 19).

1. The lower two lines of a hexagram portray its Earthy, material character or its foundation. They depict its underlying, practical, and substantive nature which exists below the surface, partly unseen, partly emerging.

2. The central two lines of the hexagram express its Humanistic qualities or its manifestation. They represent its personality and character or that which is emotional, expressed, interpersonal, and social.

3. The top two lines of a hexagram reveal its Heavenly, spiritual nature or its divine character. They represent its profoundness, that which is ethical, imperceptible, philosophical, and metaphysical.

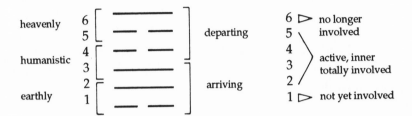

Figure 5. Basic Nature of the Six Lines

When you overlay the above pairs of lines from a hexagram onto the two trigrams that constitute that hexagram, you will observe that the top of the two central Humanistic lines is the bottom of the upper trigram. The bottom of the two central lines is the top line of the lower trigram. This means the expressed nature or dominant visible aspect does not automatically reside at the top of a trigram, but in the place closest to the *Gua*'s center.

When you comprehend the hexagram as a whole, the two trigrams are perceived as its component entities. The most visible part of the lower trigram is the top line, and the most remote is the bottom line. The most visible part of the upper trigram is the bottom line, while the most remote is the top line.

When you observe the hexagram from below as one who is about to enter its area or penetrate its field, the closest and most visible line of each trigram is its bottom line, while the most remote is its top line.

The following table can be helpful in learning some of the traditional characteristics for each line. When a hexagram has a Changing Line you can better understand those qualities that have been lost and gained. You can also see in what ways those qualities relate to the response to your inquiry, particularly with regard to the text for that particular Changing Line.

Remember, the meaning of a hexagram resides in the six lines of the *Gua* and in the *gua* as cohesive three-line symbols. The text only interprets and expresses those meanings. The text is or holds the clue to information you must comprehend, complete, and resolve within yourself. Anything that can assist in this endeavor is valuable.

LINE	TIME	ORDER	BODY	HEAD	PLANT
6 ▬ ▬ advisor sage	6th part the end the last	over- exposed preceding	head hair brain	mind intuition spirit	fruit nut seed
5 ▬▬▬ authority ruler	5th part optimum potent	encountered later, yet leading	shoulder, neck, arms, and hands	brain intellect mental	leaf flower petals
4 ▬ ▬ officer executive	4th part revealing reliable	external or exposed yet sheltered	circulation assimilation respiration	eyes appreciation emotions	branch shoots vines
3 ▬▬▬ foreman manager	3rd part transition daring	internal bordering encroaching	abdomen digestion procreative	ears enjoyment social	trunk stem
2 ▬ ▬ assistant laborer	2nd part supportive appearing	protected passive committed	buttocks, hips, knees, and thighs	nose protective material	roots sprouts
1 ▬▬▬ novice apprentice	1st part invisible potential	source arriving undecided	calf, shin, foot and toes	mouth survival physical	seed embryo germ

Figure 6. Line Qualities and Characteristics

When you have a hexagram with a Changing Line, it helps to be aware of what kind of an element is being transformed: something of a practical, material nature (lines 1 or 2); of a psychological, emotional, interpersonal character (lines 3 or 4); or of an ethical, moral, philosophical quality (lines 5 or 6). Become aware of the possible relevance of each line to your inquiry according to the symbolic references in Figure 6. For example, the Body category does not just refer to body parts or physical well being and health, but also to functions and expressions of those body parts.

Line 3 refers to "abdomen, digestion, circulation." This can be related to digesting information and ideas, or giving birth to a work of art, a business venture or a social event. Line 1, which pertains to "calf, shin, feet and toes," can easily stand for mobility or agility. Likewise, line 6, "head, hair, brain," can mean sensitizing or attuning to things.

Seek the diverse meanings of a particular line with regard to your inquiry given the hints and clues provided. Try to remain honest, impartial, and objective in applying any meaning to your inquiry. If a line is changing from yang to yin, make every effort to consider its real influence or impact. Look at both the dissolving and emerging trigrams for meaning as to the nature of the change.

Time and Timeliness

The six lines of the hexagram are cast in sequence. Thus they represent duration or the passing of time. For this reason it is usually suitable to frame your inquiry within specific time (see the sections on Casting, page 43, and Framing an Inquiry, page 70).

Generally each line represents one-sixth of the total time stated or implied in the inquiry. If an inquiry covers six months, and a Changing Line occurs in the fourth line, then that change, and the action or decision necessary to optimally bring about that change, will necessarily take place during the fourth month. The unknown lies in whether the change and the factors precipitating it will occur in the first day of the month or the last day of that month, or over a period of several days, or three to four weeks.

It is suggested that you establish a built-in "time default" for yourself. If you should frame an inquiry and inadvertently omit a time reference or constraint, this "time default" would naturally take effect. The most useful "time default" appears to be about three months, but you should find what works best for you. You can avoid the need for this if you will remember to consider and refer to time where it is a factor.

Timeliness is a factor that requires more attention than is possible here. It is mentioned to bring out awareness of it. The *I Ching* not only addresses appropriate action and ethical conduct but also constantly admonishes the reader to act in a timely fashion. Some of this is implicit, as in the Changing Lines.

Optimal results require that the protagonist conform to the time constraints as defined by the particular line. If a hexagram inquiry is designated with a two month time frame, then each line represents ten days. Any action called for or required by a specific Changing Line cannot be rushed, nor can it be procrastinated. It must be dealt with during the particular time frame as indicated by the position of that line, within the context of the time stated in the inquiry.

There are also numerous references to specific and general time throughout the *I Ching* text. Some of these have been intentionally omitted in this presentation but the implied spirit of timeliness has hopefully been preserved. Remember that timing is usually crucial and critical.

CASTING THE *I CHING*

Casting is the term used to describe the manipulation of three coins or fifty sticks to describe a *Gua* or *hexagram dynamic*. Traditionally "yarrow stalks" are used. The word *dynamic* can perhaps best depict the inherent capacity and probability of a casting to describe a hexagram that can change or transform into a different hexagram. It is theoretically possible for each cast hexagram to change into any of the other sixty-three. Some changes have a higher probability of occurring than others.

According to the *I Ching* system, theory, or philosophy, *chance* as expressed by casting is understood to respond to or resonate with natural laws and therefore conform to them as an expression of a nonconventional physics, that is, a physics of consciousness. The result or outcome is that a method of "apparent chance" defines a hexagram whose text presents a response to a stated or implied inquiry. This is a mechanism which can reflect or mirror *mind* externally.

There is a consciousness in each of us that is at one with Universal Mind/Consciousness. This may be called *metaconscious*, the all knowing within us. Unfortunately there is usually little or no communication between metaconscious mind and the conscious mind. Communication between the two is usually misunderstood, misinterpreted, or distorted by the ordinary mind's hopes and desires.

It is as though the metaconscious knows which hexagram text would provide the appropriate response or optimal perspective, both practically and ethically, when you form an inquiry. Since the metaconscious is unable to directly convey the information, and as it can not give you the name of the hexagram you should read, a casting method was devised to resolve this dilemma.

It seems as if the metaconscious mind were able to *psycho-kinetically* influence or control the "fall of the coins" or the "division of the yarrow stalks" so as to generate or indicate the necessary or appropriate hexagram. The renown psychiatrist Carl Jung, a serious student of the *I Ching*, describes this phenomenon in his famous foreword to *The I Ching*, by Richard Wilhelm.[8]

According to the intensely pragmatic Chinese, the *I Ching* will indicate in response to any inquiry, the optimal outcome, inherent limitations, the primary ethic, the necessary manner of approaching or addressing the situation, and suggestions of effective and responsible conduct under the circumstances.

Before describing the two casting methods, it is productive to explain their causal difference, which means the manner and the extent of influence metaconscious mind is able to exert over "yarrow stalks" as compared with coins.

Ritual preparation aside, you cast the coins by shaking them and letting them fall. This is a quick and simple procedure performed once for each line. By contrast you cast the stalks not by dropping, but by dividing and re-dividing. The stalk method requires more personal handling, is more time-consuming, and is composed of the light, dry remains of a living substance. It is substantially more responsive and therefore more susceptible to subtle metaconscious influence. By comparison, the coins are made of non- organic substance. Heavy, gross, and more susceptible to gravity and magnetic pull, they require more metaconscious effort and therefore a greater exertion of influence. Coins are more prone to being less synchronous or responsive to metaconscious *minding*.

The Coin Method

According to author and teacher, Da Liu, in his book *I Ching Coin Prediction*, the use of coins was introduced 2,500 years ago. He writes: "Kuei Kuo Tze . . . the great philosopher and military strategist . . . came to feel that using the yarrow stalks was too time-consuming and not suitable for the turbulent society of his day. So he devised the use of coins to replace both yarrow stalks and tortoise shells."[9]

It is said that the idea came to him in the midst of battle when he wished to consult the *I Ching* but could not afford the time needed for casting the stalks. Because his coin procedure is easier to learn and only requires a fraction of the time, it came to be the more popular method as far back as two thousand years ago. Purists and serious students have always shunned the coin method. There is however a time and place for using coins, and that is for learning, practice, and familiarization.

The coin method as devised by Kuei Kuo Tze is significantly different from the "yarrow stalk" method in its mathematical probabilities for determining Changing Lines. While this has long been known by the Chinese, it was conveniently illustrated in an article in *Scientific American* in 1974.[10] The odds of obtaining a changing yin line are $\frac{1}{16}$ with the "stalks" and $\frac{2}{16}$ with the coins. Odds for obtaining a changing yang line are $\frac{3}{16}$ with the stalks and $\frac{2}{16}$ with the coins. The Chinese surely had a reason for establishing the probabilities of the "yarrow stalk" method.

The coin method requires shaking and dropping three coins. Heads counts as "3" and tails as "2." The sum defines the value for one line. The process is repeated six times for a hexagram.

In 1976 this author resolved the mathematical inconsistency between the "coin method" and the "yarrow stalk" method. It uses three coins, but in a way that is mathematically identical with the "stalks." This by itself does not make the "coin method" identical to the "yarrow stalks" method but it should make it mathematically acceptable to traditionalists.

This *twentieth century* coin method was first reported in October 1976 in both the *East West Journal* and the *Village*

Voice. Although it has been slightly modified since then, the method has not been substantively altered.

It is recommended that the coins all be of a similar size and weight. Preferably they should be kept in a special container and wrapped in a piece of cotton, linen, or silk, to be used only with the *I Ching*. You might also consider casting the coins onto a piece of natural fabric.

1. Remove the coins from the container with attentiveness.

2. Tradition suggests you pass the coins through incense smoke to neutralize or remove any stagnant or impeding energy.

3. Cupping the three coins between your hands, take a minute or so to reflect calmly on your inquiry.

4. When you feel ready, place one of the coins to the side or secure in your fingers.

5. Keeping your attention on your inquiry or having your mind free of extraneous and distracting thoughts, shake the two coins in your hands and gently drop them or let them fall on the cloth. The coins should not be tossed casually or thrown.

Heads   Heads   Tails   Tails   Heads   Tails

Possibilities After Dropping Two Coins

6. Next, pick up one of the coins, leaving a "heads" if there is one. **Leave a "tails" only if both coins are "tails."**

7. Next, pick up the coin you originally set aside. You will now have two coins in your hand with one on the casting surface.

8. Repeat step 5, shaking the two coins and letting them fall on the cloth.

9. There are now three coins on the cloth. Add the value of the three coins counting "heads" as "3" and "tails" as "2." The sum will be 6, 7, 8 or 9. This defines the first line of the *Gua*.

10. Steps 4 to 9 are repeated for a total of six times, once for each line of the hexagram. The hexagram is constructed from the bottom to the top. This constitutes your Basic Hexagram.

T + T + T 2 + 2 + 2 = 6: the symbol is —x— **changing yin**
T + T + H 2 + 2 + 3 = 7: the symbol is —— **unchanging yang**
T + H + H 2 + 3 + 3 = 8: the symbol is — — **unchanging yin**
H + H + H 3 + 3 + 3 = 9: the symbol is —o— **changing yang**

Figure 7. Method of Counting the Coins

In Figure 7 "unchanging" means the line is stable, whereas "changing" means the line is unstable and it eventually changes to its opposite. Thus "change" is indicated by either "X" or "O" in the middle of the line. Changing yang —o— becomes a stable yin — —, and changing yin —x— becomes a stable yang ——.

As you cast each line draw it on a sheet of paper with the symbol that corresponds to the numerical total of the three coins. A sample Basic Hexagram might be the following when the values of each line cast are: 7, 9, 6, 8, 7, and 9:

These numbers indicate the value of each line in this hexagram		These numbers indicate the position of each line in every hexagram
9	———O——— 6	
7	——————— 5	
8	—— —— 4	
6	—— X —— 3	
9	———O——— 2	
7	——————— 1	

Lines 2, 3, and 6 are Changing Lines as indicated by both the "O" and the "X" as well as by the numerical values 9 and 6 to the left side of each line. This means that each 9 becomes an 8, stable, unchanging yin, and the 6 becomes a 7, stable, unchanging yang. By referring to Figure 23 on page 162 or using the I Ching Hexagram Cards, you can determine that the Basic Hexagram is 61 and the Ending Hexagram is 63.

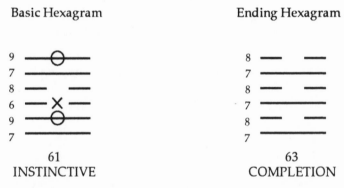

Basic Hexagram

Ending Hexagram

61
INSTINCTIVE

63
COMPLETION

Figure 8. Sample Hexagram before and after change

The Yarrow Stalk Method

The origins of this casting method are lost to history. The only thing we do know is that it came into use after the tortoise shell method of divination which prevailed over five thousand years ago. This method may seem elaborate and perhaps awkward at first, but doing it is much easier than reading about it. The method uses fifty "yarrow stalks" that should be wrapped in natural cloth such as silk, cotton, or linen, and kept in a special container and out of the way from contamination or casual handling by others. Generally a stick length of eight to sixteen inches is most comfortable to work with. But in some situations, as when traveling, small wooden sticks or toothpicks will do well. Practice the following procedure carefully and accurately. It is best to perform the manipulation of the stalks on a piece of natural cloth at least 15" x 25" which is kept folded with the stalks and used only for this purpose.

1. Remove the stalks or sticks and count them to be sure there are exactly fifty.

2. According to tradition, pass them back and forth slowly through the smoke of burning incense to purify them. Candle smoke will also do. (This step is not mandatory.)

3. Holding the sticks in your hands, take a minute or so to reflect calmly on your inquiry.

4. **Remove one of the stalks** and replace it in the container or off to the side where it is safely separated. This is called the *hexagram stick* and it remains untouched until the hexagram casting is completed.

5. Place the rest of the sticks on the cloth and divide them into two groups, randomly and without delay or deliberation.

6. Place one of the groups on the cloth at the left side and the other group on the cloth at the right side, vertically, about eighteen inches apart to avoid any possible mix-up.

7. **Remove one stick from the group on the right side** and place it on the container or on a small plate to the right of the cloth. This is called the *line stick*. It remains there until the casting for that line is completed. Then it is mixed together with the other sticks.

8. Pick up the sticks in the group at the *left* and **remove four sticks at a time** until there are four or fewer sticks remaining. There must be either 1, 2, 3, or 4 sticks. Place these at the top center of the cloth horizontally (see Figure 9).

9. Replace the sticks you removed in groups of four back in a vertical group on the left side of the cloth where they were.

10. Pick up the group of sticks on the *right* side of the cloth and **remove four sticks at a time** until there are four or fewer remaining. There must be either 1, 2, 3, or 4 sticks. Add these to the horizontal group at the top of the cloth.

11. There must be either Four or Eight sticks in the group at the top of the cloth. If the total is wrong you will want to check your counting or the total number of sticks. For novices it is most helpful to place a coin beside the sticks, "heads" if there are four sticks, "tails" if there are eight sticks. As in the Coin Method, *heads* has a value of "3" and *tails* has a value of "2." This first group of four or eight sticks represents the first of three coins for a single line cast in the Coin Method.

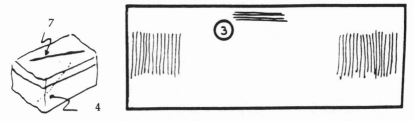

Figure 9. Yarrow Stalks After the First Division

12. Do not touch either the *hexagram stick,* the *line stick,* or the horizontal group of sticks at the top of the cloth at this time. Mix the rest of the sticks together and divide them randomly into two groups placing one group on the left and one group on the right.

13. Remove one stick from the group on the *right* and place it horizontally in the middle of the cloth.

14. Repeat step 8. Pick up the sticks in the group at the *left* and **remove four sticks at a time** until there are four or fewer sticks remaining. Place these horizontally in the *middle* of the cloth with the one stick placed there there in step 13.

15. Repeat step 9, replacing the sticks you removed in bunches of four back in a vertical group on the left side.

16. Repeat step 10. Pick up the group of sticks on the *right* side of the cloth and **remove four sticks at a time** until there are four or fewer sticks remaining.

17. When you add these to the horizontal group in the middle, there will be either four or eight sticks. Place a coin next to the sticks, "heads" for four or "tails" for eight. This second group of four or eight sticks represents the second of three coins in a single line cast in the Coin Method.

18. Do not touch either the *hexagram stick,* the *line stick,* or the two horizontal groups of sticks on the cloth. Mix the remaining sticks together and divide them randomly into two groups, placing one group on the left and one group on the right.

19. **Remove one stick from the group on the *right*** and place horizontally near the bottom of the cloth.

20. Repeat steps 14 through 17, but place the sticks in the horizontal group at the *bottom* of the cloth. Place a coin beside this bottom group, "heads" if there are four sticks or "tails" if there are eight. This third group of four or eight sticks represents the third of three coins in a single line cast in the Coin Method.

21. This segment of the casting represents the first or bottom line of your Basic Hexagram. Figure 10 should give you an idea of how things look after you have cast the first line. Counting "heads" as "$:$" and "tails" as "2" **add the total of the three coins.** You can see that a group of four sticks is considered a single yang entity, whereas as group of eight sticks is a double yin entity. As with the Coin Method, the sum of the three horizontal groups or their representative coins is either 6, 7, 8, or 9.

6 = 2 + 2 + 2: the symbol is —x— **changing yin**
7 = 2 + 2 + 3: the symbol is ——— **unchanging yang**
8 = 2 + 3 + 3: the symbol is — — **unchanging yin**
9 = 3 + 3 + 3: the symbol is —o— **changing yang**

22. Draw the line that corresponds to the sum of the three groups of sticks or the three coins on a sheet of paper. If you are using the *I Ching* Cards, place the Base Card down with correct side facing up. Then put card "1" down on top of it with the proper side facing up.

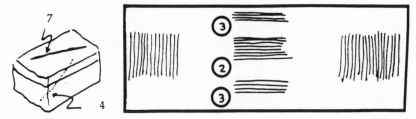

Figure 10. Yarrow Stalks After a Line is Cast

23. **Do not pick up the hexagram stick.** Pick up all the other sticks including the *line stick*, and those in the horizontal groups. You will now have forty-nine sticks in your hand.

24. Repeat steps 5 through 23 five more times for a total of six procedures, once for each line of the hexagram. Draw each line on the paper *above* the previous line.

After you do this several times, the process will become quite familiar, comfortable, and easy to remember.

Changing Lines

I Ching means "Change Classic" or "Classic of Change." A more accurate title might be "Classic of Transformation," by which is meant effecting change or harmonizing with change. If we examine the implication of this further it suggests that the *I Ching* might be the original text on strategy or the first "case study" textbook on "decision science." In the traditional context, it is a method to depict and reflect on the optimal approach to planning, decision, and action for a given condition.

There are sixty-four "hexagrams as *sets*" within the *I Ching as a system*. There is the actual possibility that any starting *set* as defined by a Basic Hexagram can transform into any other *set* as defined by an Ending Hexagram, also called a Changed Hexagram. According to traditional Chinese methods of casting, each line has a 25% probability of being a Changing Line. Therefore each hexagram has an 80% chance of having one changing line, not 150% as might appear.

A hexagram is formally generated by casting. The casting defines one of four values that are possible for each line, 6, 7, 8, or 9. The outside or extreme numbers, 6 and 9, are considered exposed and thus unstable; 7 and 8 are internal and protected, and therefore stable. In the Chinese manner, 6 is reasoned to be excessively yin or undeveloped and immature; while 9 is reasoned to be excessively yang or too old. Being unstable, they will break down or disintegrate, thereby transforming into their stable opposites: 6 changes to 7 and 9 changes to 8. They gravitate toward the center.

The function of a Changing Line is to represent or indicate that an optimal response to an inquiry and any subsequent course of action involves a shift or change from one basic framework or set of informing conditions to another. They establish that a situation is not static and that you will soon have to deal with a new set of factors. The more Changing Lines there are in a hexagram, the more unstable or variable the basic condition, and therefore the more changes you can expect to experience and deal with in regard to your inquiry. Understanding this structure can be very helpful in preparing you for most eventualities.

An example illustrating the formation of a hexagram with three Changing Lines was presented in Figure 8, page 48 in the section on "Casting The *I Ching*." The Basic Hexagram and Ending Hexagram from that example are repeated below:

Basic Hexagram   Ending Hexagram

61   63
INSTINCTIVE   COMPLETION

In this example, you would normally read the text for Hexagram 61 and then read the texts for Hexagrams 61, Lines 2, 3, and 6 in sequential order. Next you would change the three lines to their opposite, generating Ending Hexagram 63. This book presents an original theory and method for reading and understanding hexagrams with multiple Changing Lines. The process provides readers with a significant body of interpretive information not possible with the standard method. (See Transitional Hexagrams on page 64.) The Ending Hexagram represents the optimal state or best approach with regard to your inquiry within the time specified or implied.

HEXAGRAM FORMS

There are five definitive categories of hexagrams which inform every six-lined *Gua*: they are the Basic Hexagram, Nuclear Hexagram, Evolutionary Hexagram, Transitional Hexagram, and the Ending Hexagram.

Basic Hexagrams

The Basic Hexagram is usually determined by probability, cast with coins or sticks. It can be selected as simply as opening the book to a particular hexagram or reflecting on which hexagram most closely approximates or expresses your concern or inquiry. This hexagram represents the framework within which the current condition or inquiry exists. It describes the manner in which it is to be encountered and engaged. In addition, the hexagram is the point of departure from which meaningful action starts and proceeds. If there are no changing or moving lines it is the state which informs the ending condition of the inquiry.

The Basic Hexagram is the initial response to your query. It is not an answer to your question, at least not in the logical, direct, linear manner of thinking. Nor should the hexagram name or the ideas expressed or implied by a hexagram name be presumed to be or indicate any specific answer *per se*. Rather, the hexagram name and the thoughts, ideas, and concepts expressed by or through the text of that hexagram represent or reflect a mind-set or an attitude one should encompass or adopt in dealing with or addressing the question at hand.

When you cast Hexagram 55, Abundance, it is not unusual to have the idea or assume that prosperity or good fortune is inevitable or automatic. Consider the text in another light, namely how to manage, deal with, or confront your own or another person's Abundance as it relates to the inquiry. Or adopt the ethical approach or mental attitude you might have if you were to find yourself in a condition of Abundance. Lastly, consider what kind of Abundance might be intended by this hexagram with regard to your inquiry.

Using another example, people often understand Hexagram 56, Journeyer, to mean they will go traveling and they anticipate a good experience. They understand the hexagram name in a positive way. The idea, however, is to adopt the mindset of those who are authentic journeyers or travelers, of those who are out of their element, in strange or unfamiliar territory, or in an alien setting which may be awkward, difficult, or precarious. The Journeyer suggests the need to be cautious, discreet, attentive, and sensitive in unfamiliar conditions or circumstances.

Nuclear Hexagrams

The Nuclear Hexagram expresses a Basic Hexagram's essential, concealed, internal nature and qualities. It is the central, inner character or quality that one may choose to suppress or express, depending on what is deemed appropriate, desirable, or beneficial under specific circumstances. This is an historical model derived from the nucleus or middle four lines of the Basic Hexagram, lines 2, 3, 4, and 5. Lines 2, 3, and 4 form the lower nuclear trigram, whereas lines 3, 4, and 5 form the upper nuclear trigram of a Nuclear Hexagram.

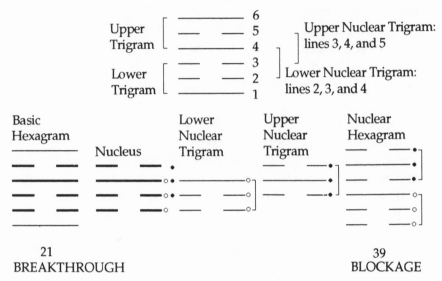

Figure 11. Forming a Nuclear Hexagram

In understanding the response to your inquiry, you should interpret the text or commentary of the Nuclear Hexagram as reflecting those qualities or forces below the level that is normally expressed. These influences are generally concealed but always present. A Nuclear Hexagram conveys the ground or that subtle nature inherent in the Basic Hexagram. It intensifies, clarifies, complements, or modifies the Basic Hexagram's text.

By knowing the Nuclear qualities and character of a Basic Hexagram, and by then acting in accord with its ideas, you will determine whether the impressions you perceive as positive or beneficial in the Nuclear Hexagram should be utilized, and whether those qualities you perceive as negative or detrimental should be suppressed. Acting contrary to the suggestions of the Basic Hexagram may suppress the positive potential and enhance the negative potential of the Nuclear Hexagram.

For example Hexagram 26, Firm Restraint, Obligations, Under Pressure, has Nuclear Hexagram 54, Formality, Convention, Customs. This suggests that when you encounter or apply Firm Restraint you are advised to submit to or conform to certain norms. Or, if and when circumstances demand, know which norms it is possible to avoid or abstain from.

Remember, that the Nuclear Hexagram name and text suggest what to be aware of or on the lookout for, and they indicate an ethical perspective to consider and embrace. It may require some reflection and effort on your part to identify or appreciate its specific relevance to your inquiry. *You do not read any of the line texts for a Nuclear Hexagram* when you are interpreting a hexagram inquiry.

Sixteen of the hexagrams are also Nuclear Hexagrams. Each of these governs four hexagrams.[11] A Nuclear Hexagram can be identified by one of four nuclear patterns. By adding a yin or yang line to the top and bottom of the following four patterns you will derive the sixteen Nuclear Hexagrams.

A.   B.   C.   D.

Figure 12. Identifying a Nuclear Hexagram

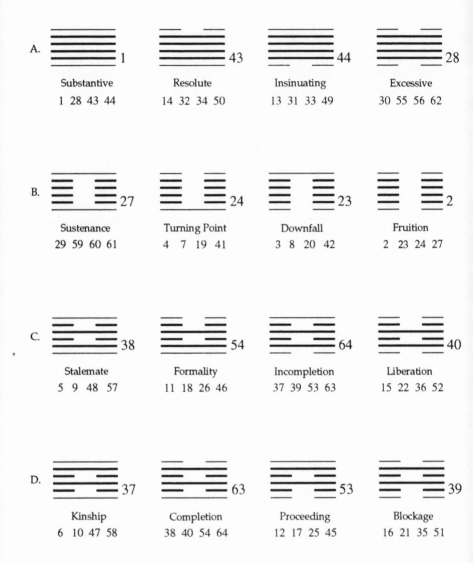

Figure 13. The Nuclear Hexagrams
The four numbers below each Nuclear Hexagram identify the four
hexagrams governed by that Nuclear Hexagram

Evolutionary Hexagrams

The Evolutionary Hexagram is an innovative hypothesis first proposed by this author in 1975. It was inspired by references in the original *I Ching* text and commentary such as, "All movements are completed in six stages, and the seventh brings return," Hexagram 24 ☷☳ , and references such as in Hexagram 44 ☰☴ , that yin "unexpectedly obtrudes again from within and below," or Hexagram 23 ☶☷ , "The yin power . . . is about to supplant the yang power altogether."[12]

This theory is also suggested or implied in an historical diagram of twelve hexagrams called the "seasonal cycle," used in ancient China for expressing and understanding the principles of medicine and agriculture, among other things (see Figure 14 cycle 1, page 63).

"Evolution" describes the natural progression of hexagram development both as a mathematical model and as a philosophical paradigm. It appears that the *I Ching* text reveals its own Evolutionary constitution. As an interpretive theory, Evolution demonstrates the manner in which hexagrams mutate as part of a *cyclical system* which in turn may be related to or inform the elusive order of the original hexagram sequence.

Evolution can be described as the "natural and eventual transformation of a hexagram"; as a set of six lines in which the bottom five lines all move up one position forcing the top line to the only remaining space, the vacated bottom position, where it changes from yang to yin or from yin to yang. When this process has repeated 12 times, a hexagram returns to itself. It becomes the starting hexagram once again.

How do we use this Evolutionary Hexagram theory in understanding and interpreting hexagrams? Depending on one's perspective or point of view, an Evolutionary Hexagram will reflect either a positive or a negative disposition. In the positive mode, the Evolutionary Hexagram acts as a "lode star," a compass setting, or a lighthouse. It serves to provide navigational guidance in the following way.

A Basic Hexagram describes a starting point but it does not usually provide a clear compass setting or sense of direction, something to head for. The Evolutionary Hexagram provides the necessary bearing, thereby serving as a beacon or reference for the Basic Hexagram. It is critical that one not become fixated on the Evolutionary Hexagram as it is always situated just beyond the reachable or attainable. It is *temptation* that is out of reach, and *fear* or *aversion* that has no concrete basis.

This raises the question about the possible negative side-effects to Evolutionary Hexagrams. These reside not in the hexagram, but in one's tendency or inclination to become entangled in a web of that hexagram's elusive attractions or its dreadful but imagined repulsions which throw one off course.

Consider that the Evolutionary Hexagram is or represents something highly desirable which appears to lie directly ahead. Instead of using it as a reference point you become totally distracted to the point of desiring to possess this. You forget that its function is solely to guide you and lose sight of your original purpose or objective.

On the other hand, perhaps it represents something that you find highly repulsive or terrible. You forget that it is nothing but a focal point which has no direct or personal affect on you, and you change direction, completely missing your destination. If you remember the function of the Evolutionary Hexagram, you will be able to cope with its temptations and distractions and you will not overreact to whatever it presents you with.

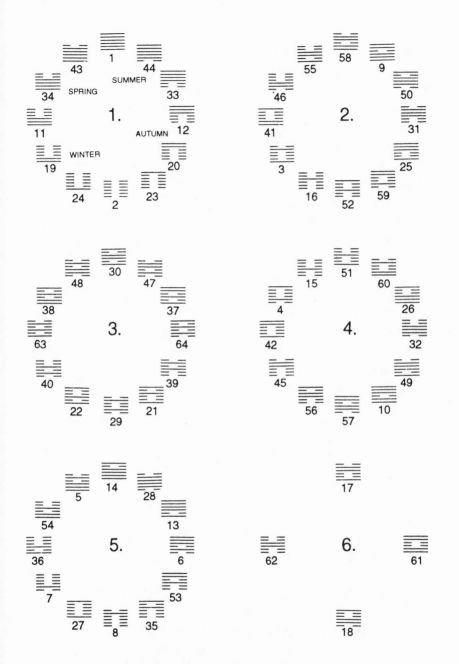

Figure 14. Evolutionary Cycles
Including the Solar Energy (Seasonal) Cycle

Transitional Hexagrams

The Transitional Hexagram is another original interpretive hypothesis developed in 1976. Unlike the preceding explanations that directly inform the essential meaning of the Basic Hexagram, this theory addresses the manner in which change or transformation transpires when a Basic Hexagram has more than one Changing Line. This is addressed more fully in Part Two, Introduction to the Hexagram Texts..

When casting a hexagram there is a possibility of generating or receiving from zero to six Changing Lines. The likelihood of getting more than three is very low. As mentioned in an earlier example, when there are three Changing Lines in a hexagram, you are instructed to read the Basic Hexagram text and then the three texts for the Changing Lines. Next you change those lines from yang to yin or from yin to yang. This defines the Ending Hexagram that you read as the condition that governs the ending period of your inquiry. It is the condition you will end up dealing with.

There is, however, something that is generally overlooked. The first Changing Line causes a fundamental modification that alters the Basic Hexagram, thereby changing it into what we call a Transitional Hexagram. At this time you would read the text for the Transitional Hexagram because it governs the subsequent period of time. The second Changing Line, although a factor or product of the Basic Hexagram is a function of this new condition expressed by the Transitional Hexagram. The second Changing Line is therefore read from the Transitional Hexagram.

The second changing line precipitates a further change that alters the Transitional Hexagram, changing it into a second Transitional Hexagram. This takes precedence over both the Basic Hexagram and the first Transitional Hexagram. The text for this second Transitional Hexagram governs the inquiry for the next period of time, until the third Changing Line takes effect.

The third Changing Line in this example is again a factor or product of both the Basic Hexagram and the first Transitional Hexagram. It is, however, a function of the second Transitional Hexagram. Therefore the third Changing Line is read from the second Transitional Hexagram.

This precipitates the last change which changes the second Transitional Hexagram into the Ending Hexagram. As above, this is read as the condition that governs the manner of dealing with ending period of your inquiry.

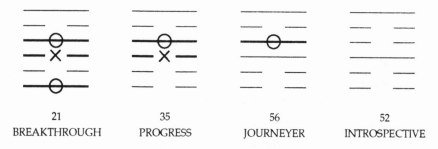

| 21 | 35 | 56 | 52 |
| BREAKTHROUGH | PROGRESS | JOURNEYER | INTROSPECTIVE |

Figure 15. Transitional Hexagram Example
with Three Changing Lines

Figure 15 illustrates that the change from Hexagram 21, Breakthrough, to Hexagram 52, Introspective, is not a sudden and instantaneous transformation or a direct transition. The three Changing Lines were cast sequentially, within the framework of time, and they will change sequentially, within that framework. What is occurring in the example is a normal, gradual, sequential transformation through two necessary transitional conditions. *Each change is a function of a different hexagram.*

By understanding the nature of the Transitional Hexagrams you gain a clearer awareness of what you are likely to relate to, experience, or have to deal with if you follow the recommended, optimal course of action given by the particular hexagram text.

For the sake of illustration, let us assume that the example of Hexagram 21, with three Changing Lines to Hexagram 52, was in response to the following question: "What benefit might I expect after six months if I were to begin this week doing regular physical exercise?"

*1. Read the text for Hexagram 21

2. Read the text for line 1 of Hexagram 21
   At the end of this text is the number [35]

*3. Read the text for Hexagram 35
   This is the first Transitional Hexagram

4. Read the text for line 3 of Hexagram 35
   At the end of this text is the number [56]

*5. Read the text for Hexagram 56
   This is the second Transitional Hexagram

6. Read the text for line 4 of Hexagram 56
   At the end of this text is the number [52]

*7. Read the text for Hexagram 52
   This is the Ending Hexagram

* indicates the four hexagrams whose texts are read.

Without a detailed analysis, you can see from the name of the Basic Hexagram that a Breakthrough is possible or forthcoming soon after beginning. Since the question includes a period of six months it is reasonable to assume that each line covers one month. There will be specific experiential changes possible in the first, third, and fourth months. The conditions that precipitate that possible change are indicated in the three line texts for Hexagrams: 21–1; 35–3; and 56–4.

1. The name of the hexagram is Breakthrough. The text of this hexagram indicates a need to be honest with yourself and others about your decision and commitment.

2. The text for Hexagram 21, Line 1 indicates the need for firm but compassionate discipline sometime during the first month. This may be imposed by a benefactor or self-discipline.

If the conditions in 1 (the Basic Text) and in 2 (the Line Text) are both met satisfactorily during the first month, then you will be drawn into the conditions expressed in Hexagram 35.

3. The name of Hexagram 35 is Progress. Therefore the preceding conditions lead to a well-defined development or improvement. The text of this hexagram indicates that continued progress depends on cooperation with a calm and competent instructor or leader. This becomes the first Transitional Hexagram.

4. The text for Hexagram 35, Line 3 indicates the need during the third month to be open to receiving encouragement or support. This is not necessarily of the gentle and kind variety. It could be difficult or come in the form of constructive criticism.

If the above conditions are met satisfactorily during the third month, then you will be drawn into the conditions expressed in Hexagram 56. This is the second Transitional Hexagram.

5. The name of Hexagram 56 is Journeyer, but this is really about deportment. It cautions one to have the conduct or behavior of one who, visiting an unfamiliar place, is prudent, careful, and more reserved than usual. You may be venturing into new territory so you are cautioned to keep a check on tendencies that could create problems or get you into difficulty.

6. The text for Hexagram 56, Line 4 indicates the need during the fourth month to not become complacent. One who would be successful in attaining his or her objective should look deeper into the purpose and meaning behind the objective.

If the above conditions are met satisfactorily in the fourth month, then you will be drawn into the conditions expressed in Hexagram 52. This is the Ending Hexagram.

7. The name of Hexagram 52 is Introspective. This indicates a state of self-reflection, acting calmly in the present moment, and becoming aware of and comfortable with your limitations.

This condition of inner focus, attention, and contemplation governs the inquiry through the remainder of the six months. Although each of the last three hexagrams supersedes or displaces the previous hexagram, it does not eliminate it. Breakthrough dissolves into Progress, which is actually a continuation of the Breakthrough. This dissolves into the Journeyer, Deportment, which governs the ongoing Progressing Breakthrough, which in turn dissolves into the Introspective, Tranquil state which evolved from the three previous hexagram conditions, all of which continue to inform this experience and development.

This approach to interpreting hexagrams requires additional time. But it is time well spent and worth the effort in that it provides you with a hexagram interpretation that is both deeper and clearer that the conventional method that skips directly from the Basic Hexagram to the Ending Hexagram with the reading of three Changing Lines from the Basic Hexagram.

It must be pointed out that the conditions or constraints of Hexagram 21, Line 4, as expressed in the text, can only apply directly to Hexagram 21 when Line 4 is the first or only Changing Line. In that case the line text is expressed as a direct function of Hexagram 21. When there is any Changing Line that occurs prior to line 4, such as in line 2, Hexagram 21 becomes modified or transformed. *It is no longer Hexagram 21, but Hexagram 21 that has changed into Hexagram 38.* In that case Line 4 is no longer a function of Hexagram 21, but of Hexagram 28.

Hexagram 21, Line 4 is no longer directly applicable to the reading, although it does retain some relevance. While it is not wrong to interpret hexagrams in the conventional way it is more accurate and beneficial to interpret hexagrams that have two or more Changing Lines according to the Transitional Hexagram method. If you compare the methods you can see the difference for yourself.

OPPOSITE HEXAGRAMS

An "Opposite Hexagram" is the hexagram whose lines are the reverse of a hexagram in questions. For example, I have named hexagram 26 ☰☰, Firm Restraint, Obligations, and Under Pressure (Mountain above pressing down and resisting and Heaven forging up from below). Its Opposite is hexagram 45 ☰☰, Assemble, a Large Convening, Planning (Lake evaporating up, above the Earth, spreading down). One way of understanding the nature of Firm Restraint is to grasp the essence of Assemble. The text describing Assemble reads "a time of enjoyable convening" and "advantage through generosity and sharing." Firm restraint is the opposite of these notions.

I have not found any mention of Opposite Hexagrams or reference to the principle of oppositeness but this is an invaluable aspect to each hexagram in that it defines in absolute terms what a Hexagram is not.

FRAMING AN INQUIRY

The key to a meaningful response is an appropriate inquiry. People usually find no problem in asking questions, but they have difficulty making appropriate inquiries. People may have more experience asking questions than any other activity. And yet it is something most of us rarely learn about in a formal way. Some historical exceptions whose traditions of teaching inquiry continues today can be found in the monastery training of Tibetan Buddhism, in the Rabbinical schools of Orthodox Judaism, and in Jesuit seminaries.

There is an art to asking questions well, and to inquiry in general. There is much truth to the adage that the answer is contained within the question. When an inquiry is a function of indecision, the desire for another perspective on a matter, for insight, for an optimum course of action, or appropriate conduct in a situation, then the response is certainly residing within the inquirer.

Most people in the West are *self* oriented. This phenomena is a function of our cultural upbringing and society. Even questions not concerning one's self, usually reflect a strong personal bias or perspective. This is not a judgment but an understanding of other cultures and social structures where one is first and foremost a member of a cohesive family or social entity as in in China, Japan, Indonesia, or most native and tribal groups.

The difference between the Orient and the West, where we also belong to meaningful or significant groups or social units, is that in the West the individual is primary, and participates in or belongs to groups that add meaning to one's life. In the Orient the group is primary.

Avoid the tendency to ask questions such as: *Should I _____? Will I/she/they _____? Can he/we _____?* These are questions that can be answered with a simple *yes* or *no*, and which leave no space for natural elaboration. Another type of inquiry that should be avoided is the "double question," such as: *Should I do _____ or _____? Will we go to _____ or _____?* Choose a single inquiry and phrase it clearly.

You may prefer to consider a variation on inquiry that looks into the thinking, reasoning, and purpose behind the question. This compels you to ask yourself why you are asking the question, who is the one that is asking the question, and why you want to have and answer. What is the real question? A few examples of more appropriate inquiries might be as follows:

1. *What would be the benefit of going to _____ next month?* This is open-ended and allows room for an indication of an outcome, obstacles, or a potential benefit, and what form these are likely to take.

2. *In what way will my career be furthered by accepting employment with _____ business, working in _____ capacity?*

3. *How can _____ person improve his or her relationship with _____ within the next two months?*

4. *What aspect of my character or behavior needs to be worked on or improved during the next year in order to _____?*

There are a few points worth noting. You will get an answer to the question you ask, not the one you meant to ask, really intended, or purposely evaded. The possible exception would be if you inquire about one thing but are totally preoccupied with another matter. It helps to keep this in mind.

A loose question begets a vague or misleading answer. You may get what you ask for, so be careful with what you request. Take responsibility for the words you choose to frame your inquiry.

As a corollary and a modification to the previously mentioned points, you want to avoid the problems that could arise by including too many conditions or too few conditions in expressing your inquiry. Examples can help clarify the pitfalls.

1. *How would it benefit me to go to _____ next summer?* If the response were Hexagram 14, Prosperity, you might assume this to be financial and make the trip. You could experience no such gain and believe the advice was all wrong. Consider that:

   a) Prosperity could come at a later time but in some way be precipitated by the trip.

   b) It could be that good-fortune would have been a different kind but your material preoccupation caused you to overlook or miss an otherwise prosperous opportunity.

   c) You did have some prosperity on or as a result of the trip but you ignored it because it did not meet your expectations.

There are surely other examples one could add.

2. You could ask a question such as: *Where can I find a business partner in the next three months who is honest, personable, cooperative, experienced, successful, outgoing, caring, and has money to invest?* Such a group of conditions might be useful for an affirmation or a "wish list." They are definitely not helpful in this

kind of an inquiry, and in fact they could be totally counterproductive.

Perhaps in the example above there is no person who can satisfy all your list of conditions in the time allowed. The *I Ching*, as a metaconscious phenomena, takes you literally. If only one quality were missing in a potential partner you would draw a blank. If you left out everything non-essential, or requested that a partner have three essential qualities, such as investment capitol, honesty, and experience, plus any three more desirable qualities you hope for, you might find several qualified people to choose from.

When you have a question that you know is acceptable, *write it down*. In this way there is no mistake about what you asked or what you meant. Where time is a (possible) factor, you are strongly urged to include this in your inquiry, whether it is a few days, a week or two, a month or a year.

It is usually best to keep the time frame of your inquiry within a year, and even better, within three to six months. At the same time, try to set a time limit that is not impractically short or unnecessarily long for the specific situation. You will not want to frame an inquiry which confines the answer to a few days when it realistically needs to be addressed within two weeks or more. As already suggested, consider a default time of not more than three months to cover those situations where you should have included a time constraint but forgot to do so.

To study the *I Ching*, or to study with the *I Ching*, is an exercise and an experience in learning about yourself. Approached properly, it can be similar to practicing certain forms of yoga, Zen koans, some types of meditation, *tai ji chuan* or Oriental brush to name a few examples. It is both practice and routine. In Chinese and Japanese, the words for a *practice* that relates to inner work is different from *practice* that involves music or sports. Unfortunately English has one word for both ideas. This leaves room for misunderstanding and confusion when these words are translated into English as "practice."

The *I Ching* is not something you "use." If anything, it is something that uses you. Working with it over a period of time will sensitize and attune you to your metaconscious, to your intuitive and subjective mind, and thus to the world around you.

Think of the exercise of casting and interpreting the *I Ching* as similar to practicing anything else. Proficiency comes from regular and repetitive exercise. The real application, the performance as it were, comes only after practice, more practice, preparation, and rehearsal.

First develop familiarity and proficiency through practice. During this time, learn to become empty of distractions and intentions or willfulness while casting and interpreting an inquiry. As part of the learning process you are encouraged to work with the *I Ching* regularly but impersonally. You can accomplish this by avoiding inquiries that are important to you personally. By limiting yourself to "learning inquiries" that are not "emotionally charged" you will develop the habit of casting the *I Ching* free of subconscious expectations and projections which could easily color or distort your interpretation of the hexagram obtained.

For practice, frame unimportant but emotionally neutral questions about friends and relatives, current events, subjects in the local news, or topics of national interest. During this learning process, where you ask questions that concern people you know, keep the interpretations to yourself. It is valuable to ask questions with a short "time frame" in order to see how your understanding compares with the actual outcome, without having to wait long for verification. Where your interpretation differs from actuality, try to understand the hexagram reading in light of what really transpired or happened, and thereby learn where or how you might have erred in your reading of the text.

It helps to remember that the more you are emotionally and intellectually empty or centered while casting with the coins or sticks, the more appropriate the hexagram you derive will be. Of course, learning to interpret accurately is an ability that comes with time. Do not be impatient. It also helps to keep a record or a journal of your readings. Write down a brief synopsis of your interpretation along with any personal comments and insights. Later you can add a note as to what actually transpired.

The use of "yarrow stalks" is highly recommended as it helps develop a meditative state of mind during the casting. When it is your main purpose to practice hexagram interpretation, do not hesitate to use the coin method to generate practice hexagrams. But definitely practice with the "yarrow stalks" and use them for making serious inquiries.

There will be occasions when you are dissatisfied with a hexagram you receive in response to an inquiry. You may be tempted to immediately, or soon after, cast another hexagram for the same question or one that is essentially the same, or varied slightly, hoping for what you think is a more favorable, more appropriate, or more meaningful hexagram reply. This attitude demonstrates a fundamental misunderstanding about both the metaconscious and the nature of the *I Ching*. It also reflects being unfocussed or uncentered during the casting.

When you ask a question over again, even if the words are changed or rearranged, you are really asking another very different question from the one written down or expressed. The real question the second time is: *I want to know why I doubt or do not (wish to) accept the original hexagram response to my inquiry.* Or it could be, *What insecurity or lack of confidence or what desires within me cause me to be dissatisfied with the initial answer to my inquiry?* So if you wish to pursue a matter beyond the initial hexagram response, then ask something directly reflecting your concerns along the lines of the examples above.

Of course if circumstances should change significantly, which rarely happens in the course of a few minutes, or if sufficient time has elapsed or passed, it could be appropriate to inquire a second time on the same subject. If you should recognize that your mood or attitude while casting the inquiry was superficial, casual, or uncentered, it could be appropriate to inquire again. In this case, such a repeated question might be phrased: *Taking into account my incorrect approach while making the initial inquiry, as well as any unknown change in conditions or circumstances, is there: a) a different response? or b)* _____*?* Select either a) or b) a variation of your own choosing. It is not advisable to make a habit of this kind of repeated inquiry.

The *I Ching* can be a very special companion at times when you do not want to cast a hexagram or make an inquiry. It can be inspiring reading for its own sake. Opening the book at random to various hexagram texts can usually draw your attention in a gentle, but perhaps firm, reminding way to something you need to consider or contemplate. It is replete with insightful ideas and significant ethics and attitudes helpful in everyday life. You will soon get an intuitive grasp and feeling for the *I Ching*. Hexagram answers or patterns will begin to form in your mind just by framing an inquiry carefully, clearly, and thoughtfully.

PART TWO

COMMENTARY

INTRODUCTION TO THE HEXAGRAM TEXTS

This section contains the concise text for each hexagram and a very brief text for each of the six individual lines. They are presented in a form that allows you to easily grasp the meaning and the idea, yet leave you a broad latitude or space in which to exercise your intuition and then complete a hexagram's thought to the extent it is relative or relevant to your inquiry.

Many profound works that have come to the West from the Orient either alienate or frustrate their readers or leave them with a false sense of comprehension and understanding. Perhaps you can remain comfortable with all the complexity and the perplexing enigma that is the *I Ching* without feeling the need to immediately understand what it is or what it means.

Its external simplicity belies its internal complexity. It is hoped that the presentation of this book will facilitate and encourage this process of exploration and self-discovery in a manner that renders your experience with the *I Ching* meaningful, challenging, and rewarding.

When you cast a hexagram, you read only the basic text. You do not read the individual line texts or incorporate their ideas into the response or your course of action unless you cast the specific line or lines with the coins or sticks. Otherwise the line texts are not read in divination or decision making.

At the end of each line text in this book there is a number. This indicates the *Changed Hexagram* that evolves when that line is the first or only one cast in that hexagram. If a line is the first of two Changing Lines, then the number indicates the Transitional Hexagram that develops, from which the Ending Hexagram will later arise. Where a line is the first of two or more Changing Lines, the number at the end of the text indicates the Transitional Hexagram that leads to another Transitional Hexagram, and thereafter up to the Ending Hexagram.

Above each hexagram text are three *Gua,* one each for the Basic, Nuclear, and Evolutionary Hexagrams. Each one includes the New Trigram Symbols which present a graphic image of the primary components and their energies for that hexagram.

Just reading the hexagram texts and contemplating the ideas presented in them can be beneficial. They can provide you with fresh perspectives that can be helpful or constructive to whatever is transpiring in your life.

The *I Ching* is an open-ended process that contributes to personal development, self-discovery, and insight. When it is misused or abused, either intentionally or accidentally there are usually built-in safeguards to protect you from your ignorance or folly. This does not mean that one can not mislead or deceive oneself or take advantage of others. But it does mean that until these tendencies are cleared up or resolved, one will be impeded from achieving optimal progress or maximum growth by virtue of these self-limiting conditions. One can even bring about reverses of fortune for oneself through the misapplication of the *I Ching*'s counsel.

The hexagram names used in this book are for the most part not exact translations from the Chinese, but words intended to convey the suggested meaning of the hexagram. In order to better communicate the idea of a hexagram name, this book uses three words for each name. To help in locating a hexagram by its name there is a hexagram name index (see page 88). The words in upper case are the primary names used in this book. Those in lower case are the names used by Richard Wilhelm. This will make it easier for those familiar with the Wilhelm book. The hexagrams are also listed in numerical order on pages 86 and 87. The names used in this book are listed first, followed by the Wilhelm name for each hexagram.

Before proceeding to the texts it would be useful to consider the *I Ching* from one other perspective, that of a Universal System that is reflecting the "Everything," and outside of or apart from which there is no *existencing*. This is the *dao* whose symbol is at the top of Figure 2, page 20.

The symbol is a two-dimensional representation of a multi-dimensional reality. Within *dao*, nothing is neutral, static, or constant. Everything is in a constant state of flux and transformation. All existence is exchanging and *interfusing* with itself in all its forms, non-forms, and anti-forms, manifesting, de-manifesting, unmanifesting, and non-manifesting. The *I Ching* is at least two overlapping and coexisting "systems." One is a binary "system" of 2 to the 6th power, containing sixty-four "sets." The other is a binary system of 2 to the 3rd power squared, in which there are eight archetypal expressions that interact with each other according to a cohesive and coherent set of laws.

The *I Ching* does not appear to be a random philosophical and divinatory exercise with some accidental or coincidental logical characteristics. Rather it seems to represent a complex system of deliberate but undeciphered logic that in turn absorbed, adopted, or embodied, and then expressed a philosophy with a fascinating predisposition for divinatory and probability characteristics.

Each hexagram is simultaneously a complete condition and a series of events or a sequencing of energies that collectively describe or reflect a category of experience. For any casting there are 64 x 64 possible outcomes, 4096 eventualities ranging from "no change," which means change that is too slow to be of current significance, to "complete change," which means total annihilation of the initial event or condition. The former occurs with relative frequency while the latter exhibits a high probability of not occurring.

The Changing Lines represent spaces and times of significant transition within a hexagram's structure or sphere of influence where change or transformation is precipitated. By interacting with or engaging a situation appropriately or inappropriately, the transformation may be modified or intensified, devastated or hastened, thereby making it better or worse. One thing is certain: the indicated change is not absolutely guaranteed where it is desired, nor is it completely avoidable when it is not desired.

The following notes are for clarification and assistance in using the commentaries or texts. If this book in any way inspires you or if it can make the *I Ching* more accessible, useful, and less confusing it might enhance the quality of your understanding and in this way serve its purpose.

Sample Layout and Interpretation

It is beneficial to develop a standard approach to writing or recording the hexagram response to your inquiry and casting. In this way it is possible to perceive information, hexagram relationships, and patterns of development. Until you devise your own recording method you might try the following system.

First write down your question at the top of a page and date it. As you are casting, draw the lines of the Basic Hexagram below the question at the top left. *Draw the lines from the bottom up* and put a "B" above it, for Basic Hexagram. Draw the trigram symbols at the right side of the upper and lower trigrams.

Draw the Nuclear Hexagram on the right and place the letter "N" above it with the trigram symbols to the right. Next to that, draw the Evolutionary Hexagram with an "H" above and its trigram symbols to the right. The three hexagrams will cover the left half of the page, leaving the right side for notes and comments. Below each of the hexagrams, write the hexagram number and name. If there are no Changing Lines, you will not draw any additional hexagrams. If there is one

Changing Line, you will draw the Ending Hexagram below the Basic Hexagram. Then on the right side you will draw its Nuclear and Evolutionary Hexagrams.

When there is more than one Changing Line you will have to draw the Transitional Hexagram(s) below the Basic Hexagram, together with each one's Nuclear and Evolutionary Hexagram. It is best to draw the trigram symbols. Write your comments on the text and, below that, any comments you need to make for Changing Lines.

For each Basic or Transitional Hexagram you read only one Changing Line. When you cast *two Changing Lines*, the first or lowest is read for the Basic Hexagram, the second is read for the Transitional Hexagram. These change into the Ending Hexagram. You include the line texts in a reading *only* when you receive Changing Lines in the casting. Otherwise the Changing Line texts are not relevant to a hexagram reading. Figure 16 on page 85 provides a sample or model for recording hexagram readings.

A *Basic Hexagram* articulates the ground or framework within which to comprehend or engage the primary universal condition represented by your inquiry. The response to your inquiry begins with one of the sixty-four hexagram archetypes which will deal with the particular inquiry and its related conditions. Where applicable, this is addressed within a specified or implied time.

The *Six Appended Line Texts* for each hexagram depict and explain the primary avenues of transformation that prescribe the change of one hexagram into another hexagram. A Basic Hexagram can change into any other hexagram but it must first pass through one of its six primary "connecting hexagrams" represented by the six lines. These establish particular dynamics that transform the Basic Hexagram into another hexagram identified by the number at the end of the line text. A Hexagram cannot change into another without first passing through one of these six.

The *Nuclear Hexagram* indicates a hexagram's inner character or personality. It is a quality or resource you may want to foster, express, or utilize, or one that you may prefer to conceal, restrain, or hold in check depending on the specific conditions and your particular needs and inclinations.

The *Evolutionary Hexagram* indicates where a Basic Hexagram is normally heading. It provides a compass setting and direction. As such it represents a point of reference and a course that may be used to advantage in deciding how to proceed from or through the Basic Hexagram. The Evolutionary Hexagram also indicates possible distractions or temptations. These can easily be dealt with or avoided when they are recognized and understood.

Sample Hexagram Layout

It is beneficial to develop a regular method of setting down the hexagrams and notes in a reading. This way it is possible to see patterns, development, and information. Adapt the model on the next page to your own style and needs.

First, write your inquiry at the top of the page. Below, draw the Basic Hexagram and trigram symbols. To the right draw the Nuclear Hexagram, with its number and name below. Below this write the Evolutionary Hexagram name and number.

After this follow the pattern in the example, drawing any Transitional Hexagram(s) with its Nuclear Hexagram, ending with the Changed Hexagram. Remember, below each one write the Evolutionary Hexagram and its number.

When you have completed the layout, get a feeling for what it represents, more as a process than as a specific answer. Read the appropriate hexagram texts and write key points on the right side. At the bottom of the page make a note of any thoughts you have on the inquiry even if they don't seem relevant. Later, make a note of how the events actually unfold.

DATE:
QUESTION: (for example: during the next six weeks, how may I improve my relationship with my business associate[s] to optimize our personal fulfillment and financial rewards or renumeration?)

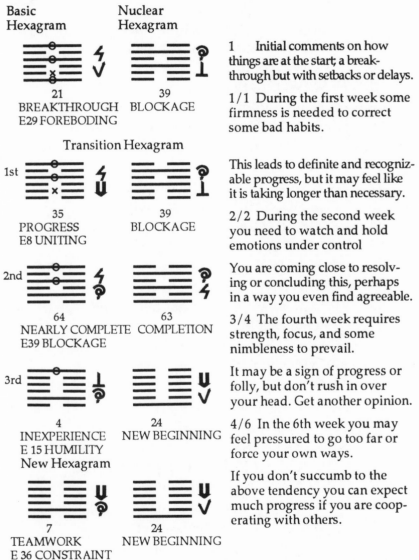

Basic Hexagram

21
BREAKTHROUGH
E29 FOREBODING

Nuclear Hexagram

39
BLOCKAGE

1   Initial comments on how things are at the start; a breakthrough but with setbacks or delays.

1/1 During the first week some firmness is needed to correct some bad habits.

Transition Hexagram

1st

35
PROGRESS
E8 UNITING

39
BLOCKAGE

This leads to definite and recognizable progress, but it may feel like it is taking longer than necessary.

2/2 During the second week you need to watch and hold emotions under control

2nd

64
NEARLY COMPLETE
E39 BLOCKAGE

63
COMPLETION

You are coming close to resolving or concluding this, perhaps in a way you even find agreeable.

3/4 The fourth week requires strength, focus, and some nimbleness to prevail.

3rd

4
INEXPERIENCE
E 15 HUMILITY
New Hexagram

24
NEW BEGINNING

It may be a sign of progress or folly, but don't rush in over your head. Get another opinion.

4/6 In the 6th week you may feel pressured to go too far or force your own ways.

7
TEAMWORK
E 36 CONSTRAINT

24
NEW BEGINNING

If you don't succumb to the above tendency you can expect much progress if you are cooperating with others.

1/1: First changing line/line ONE   3/4: Third changing line/line FOUR

Figure 16. Sample Inquiry and Hexagram Layout with Four Changing Lines

Hexagrams Listed In Numerical Order

1. SUBSTANTIVE, creative
2. FRUITION, receptive
3. INITIAL DIFFICULTY
4. INEXPERIENCED, youthful folly
5. PAUSING, waiting (nourishment)
6. DIVISIVE, conflict
7. TEAMWORK, the army
8. UNITING, holding together (union)
9. HINDRANCE, taming power of the small
10. AUDACITY, treading (conduct)
11. MERGING, peace
12. SEPARATION, standstill (stagnation)
13. RELATIONSHIP, fellowship with men
14. PROSPERITY, possessions in great measure
15. HUMILITY, modesty
16. INSPIRATION, enthusiasm
17. FOLLOWING, adapting
18. REPAIR, work on what has been spoiled
19. OPPORTUNITY, approach
20. COMPOSURE, contemplation (view)
21. BREAKTHROUGH, biting through
22. ADORNMENT, grace
23. DOWNFALL, splitting apart
24. TURNING POINT, return
25. NATURALNESS, innocence (the unexpected)
26. FIRM RESTRAINT, taming power of the great
27. SUSTENANCE, corners of the mouth
28. EXCESSIVE, preponderance of the great
29. FOREBODING, abysmal, water
30. ATTACHMENT, the clinging, fire
31. RESPONSIVE, influence (wooing)
32. ENDURING, duration

33. WITHDRAWAL, retreat
34. POWERFUL, the power of the great
35. PROGRESS, improvement
36. CONSTRAINT, darkening of the light
37. KINSHIP, the family (the clan)
38. STALEMATE, opposition
39. BLOCKAGE, obstruction
40. LIBERATION, deliverance
41. DECREASE, loss
42. INCREASE, gain
43. RESOLUTE, break-through (resoluteness)
44. INSINUATING, coming to meet
45. ASSEMBLE, gathering together (massing)
46. STRIVING, pushing upward
47. ADVERSITY, oppression (exhaustion)
48. SOCIETY, the well
49. REVOLUTION, molting
50. CIVILIZATION, the caldron
51. PROVOKING, the arousing, thunder (shock)
52. INTROSPECTIVE, keeping still, mountain
53. PROCEEDING, development (gradual progress)
54. FORMALITY, the marrying maiden
55. ABUNDANCE, fullness
56. JOURNEYER, the wanderer
57. PERMEATING, the gentle, wind (penetrating)
58. PLEASURE, the joyous, lake
59. DISPERSION, dissolution
60. LIMITATION, restriction
61. INSTINCTIVE, inner truth
62. RESTRAINED, preponderance of the small
63. COMPLETION, after completion
64. INCOMPLETION, before completion

Hexagrams Listed in Alphabetical Order [13]

90

receptive [2]
RELATIONSHIP [13]
REPAIR [18]
RESOLUTE, resoluteness [43]
RESPONSIVE [31]
RESTRAINED [62]
retreat [33]
return [24]
REVOLUTION * [49]
SEPARATION [12]
shock, thunder [51]
SOCIETY [48]
splitting apart [23]
stagnation [12]
STALEMATE [38]
standstill [12]
STRIVING [46]
SUBSTANTIVE [1]
SUSTENANCE [27]
taming power of the great [26]
taming power of the small [9]
TEAMWORK [7]
trouble [39]
TURNING POINT * [24]
treading [10]
unexpected, the [25]
UNITING, union [8]
view [20]
waiting [5]
wanderer, the [56]
well, the [48]
willing submission [57]
WITHDRAWAL [33]
wooing [31]
work on what has been spoiled [18]
youthful folly [4]

GUIDE TO THE HEXAGRAM TEXTS

A. The hexagram number

B. The six lines of the hexagram or *Gua*

C. The hexagram name in *pinyin* romanization[14]

D. The primary hexagram name in English

E. The two supporting hexagram names

F. The hexagram name in Chinese characters

G. The Basic Hexagram lines with trigram symbols

H. The Basic Hexagram number identified by the letter "B" and its name

I. The Nuclear Hexagram and its trigram symbols

J. The Nuclear Hexagram number identified by the letter "N" and its name

K. The Evolutionary Hexagram and its trigram symbols

L. The Evolutionary Hexagram number identified by the letter "E" and its name

M. The commentary or text for the Basic Hexagram

N. The individual texts for the six lines of the Basic Hexagram where #1 is the lowest or first and #6 is the highest or last

P. The number at the end of each line indicates the New or Changed Hexagram when that line is the first or only Changing Line cast for the hexagram

Q. The circle ○ next to a line number indicates that line governs the hexagram, meaning it has primary significance or is pivotal in a strategic way

R. A square ☐ next to a line number indicates that line has primary significance in a social or relational way

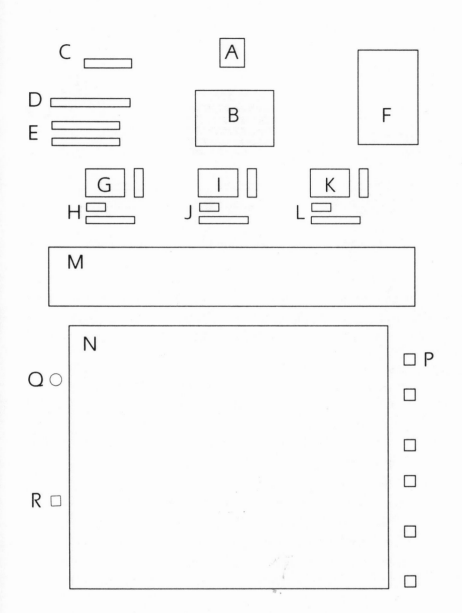

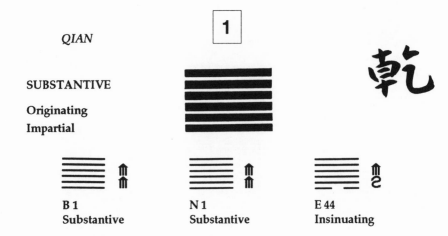

QIAN

1

SUBSTANTIVE

Originating
Impartial

B 1	**N 1**	**E 44**
Substantive	Substantive	Insinuating

Success depends on being resolute, unswerving and impartial. Take charge and put order into your affairs. You will be positively transformed by completing everything you start. Substantive actions will prove to be most fulfilling.

1. Restrain yourself. It is premature for taking action. It would be ineffective or wasted. Remain calm and patient.   44

2. Be committed to pursuing this with seriousness and integrity. Avoid ostentation or pretension and seek counsel.   13

3. Act with integrity and composure. Do not be over-whelmed by problems or let success go to your head.   10

4. This is a time of uncertainty and transformation; a time to be outgoing or to choose quiet, privacy, and seclusion.   9

○ 5. Your influence can be significant and spread widely. Obtain advice. Become harmonious with circumstances and people.   14

6. You are cautioned against going too far and losing what you already have. A moderate appetite will prevent regret.   43

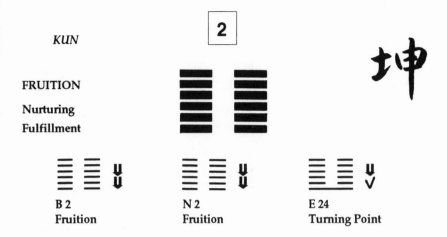

KUN

| 2 |

FRUITION

Nurturing
Fulfillment

B 2
Fruition

N 2
Fruition

E 24
Turning Point

坤

Proceed slowly. Defer your own ideas, initiative, and ambition. At this time it is best to be practical and follow sensibly. Help others in their pursuits and employ quiet or gentle s‛rength to guide or move others to assume responsibility for their actions.

1. Become sensitive and learn to recognize what is forthcoming. You can alter the course. You will reap what you sow. 24

○ 2. Be stable and strong without being willful. Remain in your element. Prosperity comes in its own proper time. 7

3. Let others enjoy recognition and glory. Be concerned only with competently completing everything that you start. 15

4. Avoid difficulty by remaining attentive. Dissipate potential hostility with self-restraint by keeping a low profile. 16

5. Be appreciative for the "good" you have. Conduct yourself with discretion, sincerity, dignity, and grace. 8

6. If you become too ambitious, greedy, or insistent you will lose out or become diminished in the ensuing conflict. 23

ZHUN

INITIAL DIFFICULTY

Struggle
Formulation

B 3
Initial Difficulty

N 23
Downfall

E 41
Decrease

Strengthen and organize your present position or direction. Odds are not favorable for starting something new at this time under present circumstances. It would help to get third-party advice or aid. With persistence and self-restraint you can expect success.

○ 1. Remain focused on your objective. Take your time, obtain help, and get things organized, avoiding any use of force.   8

2. Be extremely selective if you accept help, especially when in difficulty. Be patient; a mistake would be costly.   60

3. Unless you have the proper help to extricate yourself, accept the situation and remain calmly where you are.   63

4. When something is beyond your personal capability, get help. This may require initiative and humility on your part.   17

○ 5. When misunderstandings and interruptions block you, progress is still possible with a slow, steady, quiet effort.   24

6. Many people would give up when overwhelmed by difficulty. With courage you can ultimately prevail.   42

MENG

4

INEXPERIENCED

Uninformed
Ignorant

B 4
Inexperienced

N 24
Turning Point

E 15
Humility

Recognize your limitations. It is time to get counsel or instruction. Seriously consider the advice you receive. Do not discard what you do not want to hear. Only a fool mistakes good luck for wisdom. It is unwise to make the same request over and over.[16]

1. Some direction and discipline are appropriate and necessary, but if too overbearing these can be counter-productive. 41

○ 2. Confront inexperience, folly, and immaturity with tolerance and strength. They indicate maturity and responsibility. 23

3. Avoid close relationships with those who lack self-control, composure, and dignity. Nothing good would result. 18

4. It is sometimes necessary to undertake irrational or foolish pursuits just to experience failure or humiliation. 64

○ 5. When inexperience or innocence is combined with humility and a willingness to learn, everyone will benefit. 59

6. Two wrongs do not make a right. When discipline is required, it must be applied constructively and without anger. 7

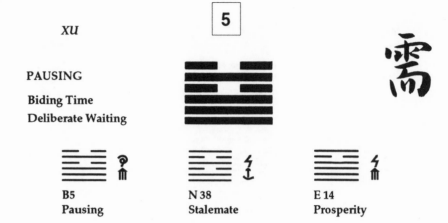

xu

5

PAUSING

Biding Time
Deliberate Waiting

B5	**N 38**	**E 14**
Pausing	Stalemate	Prosperity

Do not take any specific action. You could get in over your head, act indiscriminately, and become easily distracted from what is important. Only patience, strength, and avoiding rash action can overcome difficulty. Start something different or wait this out.

1. When difficulty is in the distance do not go to confront it. Conserve your energy, stay alert, and carry on as usual. 48

2. Instability and dissension can bring one to the brink of conflict or the brunt of slander. Just stay calm. 63

3. When you are in an exposed, compromising, or vulnerable position, only exceptional caution can prevent harm. 60

4. If you are stuck in the midst of peril or jeopardy, remain confident and composed and flow with the situation. 43

○ 5. Even in times of intense difficulty there are relaxing pauses. Enjoy these moments to recoup energy and refocus. 11

6. No matter how difficult the circumstances or conditions, it is fortuitous to remain gracious and hospitable. 9

SONG

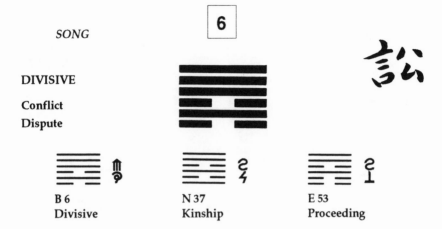

6

DIVISIVE

Conflict
Dispute

訟

B 6	N 37	E 53
Divisive	Kinship	Proceeding

Some discord is inevitable in most relationships. Progress is at hand so do not leave or change course. Sincere compromise and flexibility can resolve issues amiably. Nevertheless it is best to consider counsel or advice from a third (disinterested) party.

1. While a conflict is still under control and not yet "out of hand," it can end well if the friction is not aggravated.   10

2. In confronting a superior adversary it is honorable and wise to retreat, thereby averting harm for all concerned.   12

3. This is no time to seek distinction. With perseverance you can resolve initial problems that conceal good fortune.   44

4. Conflict is not a way to resolve turmoil and discontent. It is possible, however, through peaceful acceptance.   59

○ 5. Seriously consider binding arbitration or mediation. If your conscience is clear, you have nothing to lose.   64

6. Success that is achieved through unjust or violent means may gain some credit but not bring any peace or pleasure.   47

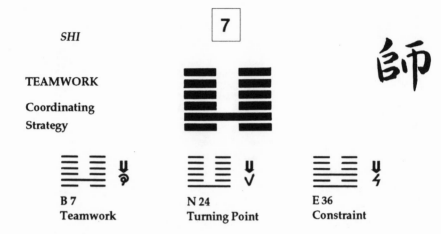

SHI

TEAMWORK

**Coordinating
Strategy**

7

師

B 7
Teamwork

N 24
Turning Point

E 36
Constraint

With collective action or joint effort, nothing stands in your way. If you are fair, ethical, and not overbearing, others will aid and support your objectives. If the person leading does not abuse his or her position, a good outcome can be expected.

1. Expect disruption or failure if things are not in order or if your associates are not coordinated or cooperating. 19

○ 2. Your affairs will not be managed well from a distance or if no one has clear authority. Benefit everyone you serve. 2

3. Misfortune results when correct order is interrupted. Some things can not be managed effectively by committee. 46

4. There are times when it is strategically wise to retreat. There is neither shame nor blame in such a decision. 40

○ 5. At no time must a breakdown in organization or direction be permitted. The results would be disastrous. 29

6. Everyone participating in a success must be fairly rewarded and credited according to their contribution and ability. 4

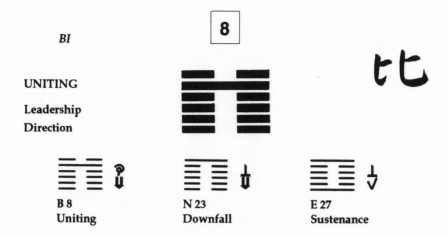

BI

8

UNITING

Leadership
Direction

B 8
Uniting

N 23
Downfall

E 27
Sustenance

If you are capable of handling responsibility, then lead others in a collective undertaking. Otherwise, subordinate your personal desires and join in a common endeavor. Do not procrastinate or you will miss a truly rewarding opportunity or accomplishment.[17]

1. Productive or meaningful relationships will develop when integrity, honesty, and sincerity bind and strengthen them.   3

2. You will gain nothing by ingratiating yourself to others. Persevere in maintaining your dignity and self-esteem.   29

3. In befriending the wrong kind of people you will suffer by alienating yourself from your real friends and allies.   39

4. You are obviously close to those at the center of action or power. Remain true to yourself and do not stray.   45

○ 5. People must cooperate with or work for each other willingly. Always provide yourself and others with a way out.   2

6. Valuable opportunities will be lost if one is not strong or clear-minded. You would regret being indecisive.   20

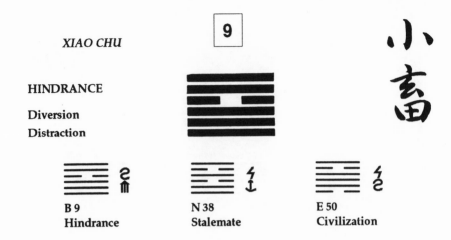

XIAO CHU

HINDRANCE

Diversion

Distraction

B 9
Hindrance

N 38
Stalemate

E 50
Civilization

Distraction or temptation can temporarily hold you in check. Your progress will be achieved harmoniously and more rapidly if you are gentle and soft. Force cannot succeed, so be patient. Do not become rattled or confused. This condition will not last.

1. Any effort will meet with resistance. Recover and choose an approach that offers some options and flexibility.   57

2. Although proceeding is desirable, it is obviously hazardous or risky. Do not give yourself any unnecessary exposure.   37

3. You can easily underestimate or miscalculate the obstacles. Advancing causes conflict or turmoil and sets you back.   61

☐ 4. With some good advice and positive influence you have a chance to avert disaster. Remain objective and honest.   1

○ 5. Real strength lies in genuine, sincere, mutually supportive reciprocity. Share the resulting benefits joyfully.   26

6. You may have accumulated considerable merit but do not push your luck. Certain external influences could be negative.   5

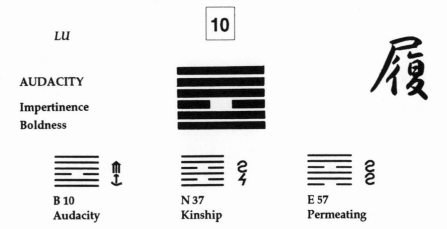

LU

AUDACITY

Impertinence
Boldness

B 10
Audacity

N 37
Kinship

E 57
Permeating

Be discerning or you might inadvertently exceed the limits of acceptable conduct. Even though one may tread incautiously it is not unreasonable to take a chance or a risk. You can succeed in a precarious situation by not abusing kindness or forbearance.

1. You are a free agent and can pursue any course that does not impose on others. Do not become preoccupied with success.   6

2. Find contentment in a peaceful, inner path without obscurations. Avoid temptation and become self-sufficient.   25

☐ 3. By ignoring your limitations and shortcomings you will court disaster. Only an exceptional event might justify this.   1

4. You may tread a precarious and dangerous path if you are absolutely confident, prudent, and extremely cautious.   61

○ 5. You must abide in the awareness of a continuing or impending danger. Persist only if you have virtue and fortitude.   38

6. The nature and results of your actions speak for themselves. And the consequences will be consistent with them.   58

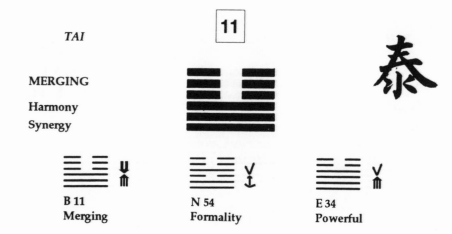

TAI

MERGING

Harmony
Synergy

B 11
Merging

N 54
Formality

E 34
Powerful

Harmony, peace, unity, or a meaningful intimate relationship require maturity, strength, and calm as well as commitment. Expect prosperity and success if you manage your natural resources well. Remain grounded and do not (try to) manipulate or mislead others.

1. When your principles and abilities are well grounded, your actions achieve much toward the well-being of others. 46

○ 2. Complete your own tasks and carry your own burdens. Remain steadfast, considerate, forbearing, and generous. 36

3. Enjoy what you have sensibly. Nothing lasts forever. Good and bad, prosperity and decline, all have their cycles. 19

4. Be comfortable and genuine with people from all walks of life. Those who are virtuous can be either rich or poor. 34

○ 5. In some activities, exchanges, or relationships it is best to not measure the equality of things but the equitability. 5

6. When conditions are disintegrating, accept the inevitable. To resist could be devastating. Stick by your friends. 26

PI

SEPARATION

Standstill

Pulling Apart

否

B 12	N 53	E 20
Separation	Proceeding	Composure

Where a lack of communication leads to chaos, disunion, or disharmony, things could reach an impasse or a deadlock. Do not be tempted or compromised. Withdraw and find strength within. Good intentions will be misunderstood, so do not even try.

1. Use your influence to lead others wisely to inner values and understanding rather than into outer accomplishments. 25

☐ 2. You must remain calm and unentangled, even when restrained by the demands of those who require help and attention. 6

3. Those who grasp more than they can handle come to realize their incapability. Their disgrace is a healthy sign. 33

4. To direct others in a change for the better, one must be competent, confident, authoritative, and unpretentious. 20

○ 5. When an improvement is occurring, the transition can be shaky and even precarious. Be cautious and not overconfident. 35

6. To bring about an end to difficulty and still maintain peace requires effort, ability, and appropriate timing. 45

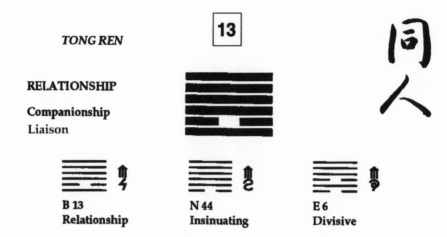

TONG REN

13

同人

RELATIONSHIP

Companionship
Liaison

B 13
Relationship

N 44
Insinuating

E 6
Divisive

Relationships flourish when there are no ulterior motives and nothing is hidden. Discernment and cooperation lead to success. Modest guidance, management, or administration brings a willing unity. Persistence in a new enterprise can be beneficial.

1. Before starting seriously, first get together congenially. This sharing will prevent later hostility and friction. 33

○ 2. Avoid becoming involved with those who limit their relating due to prejudice or selfishness. It is truly shameful. 1

3. Alienation arises when there is suspicion, doubt, insecurity, or distrust. A resolution, however, looks very promising. 25

4. The barriers that divide may be approached but not yet crossed. Ultimately conflict will end quite beneficially. 37

☐ 5. Wishing for harmony but experiencing separation is cause for anguish. Joyful resolution, however, appears with faith. 30

6. Your ideal of a relationship may be missing, but open up. It is rewarding to establish friendships with those nearby. 49

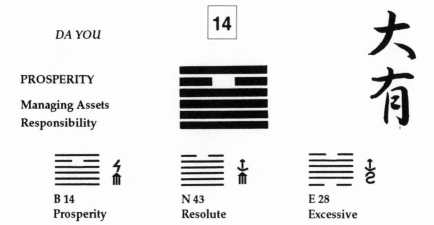

DA YOU

14

大有

PROSPERITY

Managing Assets
Responsibility

B 14
Prosperity

N 43
Resolute

E 28
Excessive

The unpretentious leader or manager maintains authority and power by strengthening and enriching supporters. Remain humble and maintain a clear goal or objective. Accentuate the positive and eradicate the negative. This will precipitate substantive results.

1. One can not be faulted for having abundance, only for abusing it. Avoid erring by remaining aware of the obstacles. 50

2. It is a waste and a shame to have something of value and not to put it to good use. Get help to accomplish this. 30

3. It takes an outstanding person to benefit others by sharing personal prosperity. Most people are miserably possessive. 38

4. Remember, you are but a custodian of all you have. Flaunting it creates unproductive, unnecessary rivalry and jealousy. 26

○ 5. Dignity, kindness and generosity attract others who are also sincere. But do not let them take anything for granted. 1

6. Recognize a greater cause as the source of your supply. Remain truthful, humble, thankful, loving, and faithful. 34

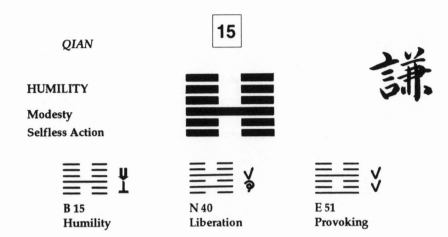

QIAN

15

HUMILITY

Modesty
Selfless Action

謙

B 15
Humility

N 40
Liberation

E 51
Provoking

To obtain a clear perspective, balance your values and order your life. Moderate your needs and avoid greed, the meek shall inherit. When you reduce excesses and augment your deficits, you can be certain that improvement and accomplishment will arrive soon.

1. Deal with difficult undertakings modestly and efficiently. Do not prolong things or make a big issue out of them.   36

2. Speak from your heart and say what you feel. Let your action be a natural, spontaneous expression of yourself.   46

○ 3. Things won't get completed if you are fatigued or distracted. Do not let the possibility of distinction go to your head.   2

4. Fulfill your obligations and avoid false modesty. Respect those above and give credit to those who assist you.   62

5. One charged with responsibility must be humble and behave impartially, but in an authoritative or decisive manner.   39

6. Act according to your beliefs. If you are at odds with those in power, then vigorously proceed to set things right.   52

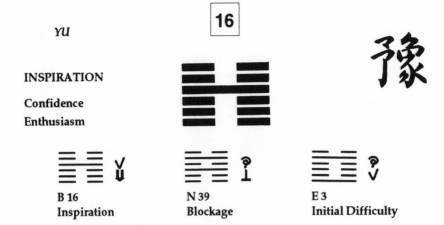

YU

16

INSPIRATION

Confidence
Enthusiasm

B 16
Inspiration

N 39
Blockage

E 3
Initial Difficulty

Your charisma spontaneously stirs others to pursue inner work or follow a calm and just manager or director in a new venture. Promotions must be deserved and penalties fair. An open heart and mind will bring fulfillment. Use your creative talents.

1. Enthusiasm that serves to promote, glorify, or aggrandize oneself is an imprudent abuse that becomes one's downfall. 51

2. One who sees things realistically is not impressed by what is merely external. Remain firm, objective, and composed. 40

3. It is helpful to look to another for inspiration. But do not hesitate or you will later regret missing an opportunity. 62

○ 4. One who is confident and self-assured becomes truly magnetic and inspiring, thereby attracting others to cooperate. 2

5. If your eagerness is blocked, it is a blessing in disguise. A more concerted effort can turn this condition around. 45

6. Enthusiasm leads to self-deception. It can end well if you recognize this in time to make the necessary changes. 35

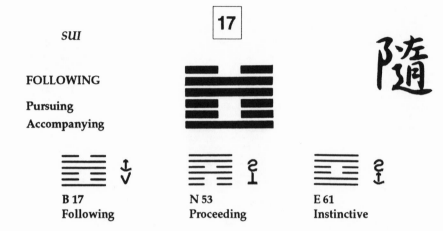

SUI

17

FOLLOWING

Pursuing
Accompanying

B 17
Following

N 53
Proceeding

E 61
Instinctive

隨

Set aside personal desires, as they will impair your judgment. Do not get distracted. Adaptability is required. To know how to lead one must first learn to serve. Harmony with others brings much success without error or problems, so relax and lighten up.

○ 1. Alter your usual approach and extend yourself. Become more receptive to alternative ideas, opinions, and attitudes.   45

2. You cannot be in two places at one time. Do not give up something of substance for another of doubtful worth.   58

3. After making a significant change for the better, you may experience some misgivings or a sense of loss. No regrets!   49

4. Do not become trapped by your ego. Distance yourself from those seeking personal gain and pursue a coherent path.   3

○ 5. Whatever objective, incentive, or higher ideal inspires you, it is beneficial to follow it with dedication.   51

6. Where there is awareness and a commitment to learn or follow sincerely, one receives the appropriate teaching.   25

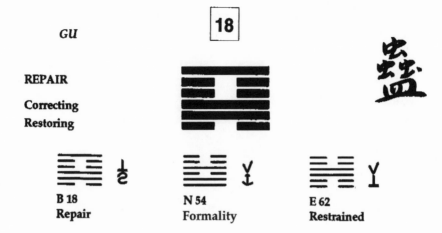

GU

18

REPAIR

Correcting
Restoring

B 18
Repair

N 54
Formality

E 62
Restrained

Decay comes about due to neglect or abuse. This time is a turning point and an opportunity to restore what has deteriorated. Pay attention, take initiative, and get to the root of things. What was before can be again. The effort is rewarding in itself.

1. You may have inherited the problem but it is up to you to repair the situation. It is difficult but restorable. 26

2. Problems due to careless indifference or error require a thorough, sensitive, easy approach, not a harsh one. 52

3. Trying too hard or overcompensating adds irritation to an existing imbalance. Still, it is better than too little. 4

4. If what must be mended is procrastinated or avoided due to indifference or laziness, disgrace is sure to follow. 50

○ 5. If you cannot resolve this alone, then with the assistance of others you can certainly obtain commendable results. 57

6. You can only justify non-involvement in these temporal affairs if you are truly dedicated to a more noble cause. 46

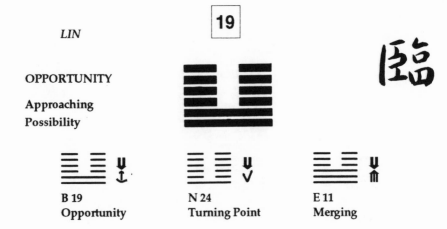

LIN

OPPORTUNITY

Approaching
Possibility

B 19
Opportunity

N 24
Turning Point

E 11
Merging

When approaching a new plateau of responsibility, awareness, or personal potential, be selfless in your sharing or giving and patient in your resolve. Make the best of this auspicious time while it lasts. Then opportunity and your success are assured.

○ 1. Progress is made when all concerned coordinate their efforts. It is imperative that you hold firmly onto your values. 7

○ 2. Remain centered, knowing that whether affairs appear to be improving or declining, they are supporting your growth. 24

3. Do not become aloof or take things for granted. Check this tendency before it undermines a good relationship. 11

4. When helping or serving others less capable it is auspicious to limit them only by their ability and principles. 54

5. Whoever is in charge will attract competent subordinates by delegating responsibility and granting authority. 60

6. A special opportunity arises when those with vast experience offer to share what they know and understand selflessly. 41

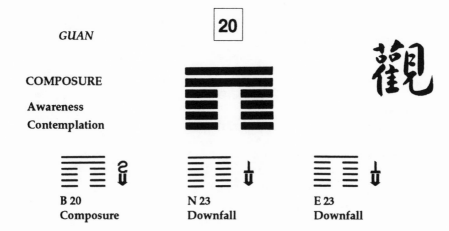

GUAN

20

COMPOSURE

Awareness
Contemplation

B 20
Composure

N 23
Downfall

E 23
Downfall

You can be an example for others. Dignity and sincerity combined with insight will inspire respect. Look around and within for direction. The gates to transformation are open so remain flexible and responsive. Accept ethical and experienced counsel.

1. Do not be satisfied with superficial or distant involvement. Take the initiative, get active, and set an example.   42

2. Apprehension and insecurity limit you to a narrow, personal point of view. This will deter or harm only yourself.   59

3. To see the results your actions have (had) on both yourself and others, broaden and deepen your perspective.   53

4. One who has something exceptionally valuable to offer must be given independence and the opportunity to share it.   12

○ 5. Whoever accepts the responsibility of becoming an example to others must regularly evaluate his or her influence.   23

○ 6. Forget yourself for a short while. It is time to consider those affairs that are beyond your personal concern.   8

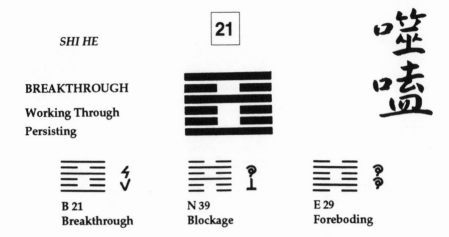

SHI HE

BREAKTHROUGH

**Working Through
Persisting**

B 21
Breakthrough

N 39
Blockage

E 29
Foreboding

The way to harmony and unity is blocked, thwarted, or frustrated by dishonesty and deceit. Confront and resolve such situations quickly, firmly, fairly, and legally if necessary. Improvement is achieved either by splitting apart or becoming closer.

1. One whose vices, misdeeds, or wrongdoings have not yet become habitual requires firm but compassionate discipline. 35

2. Do not respond to repeated offenses with anger and thereby inflict too severe a retribution, even if it is fair. 38

3. When a wrong continues unchecked, there is resentment if one without authority assumes the necessary disciplining. 30

4. You can prevail and triumph in the arduous task of opposing injustice if you are direct and have fortitude. 27

○ 5. One who tends to be tolerant finds it difficult to make the necessary decisions. The evidence however, demands action. 25

6. One who continually transgresses and always refuses to heed admonition will soon suffer humiliating misfortune. 51

BI

ADORNMENT

Embellish
Elegance

貴

B 22
Adornment

N 40
Liberation

E 40
Liberation

Clear up current matters and pursue a new project. Modest aims will succeed but significant endeavors will be misunderstood. Be yourself. Know the difference between essence and appearance, real and superficial. Your inner character will shine elegantly.

1. You will make more progress and convey elegance by not choosing a short-cut or comfortable, effortless approach. 52

○ 2. If you plan to spend time and energy on appearances, at least see that they accurately reflect inner substance. 26

3. Good fortune can be so enjoyable and pleasant that it will overwhelm and intoxicate you with self-indulgence. Beware! 27

4. When confronted by a choice between something quiet and unaffected or outgoing and elegant, select the former. 30

5. You are best to disassociate from those whose primary concerns are materialistic. What you value is elsewhere. 37

○ 6. You may comfortably eliminate all behavior and appearances that are not a function or expression of your essence. 36

BO

DOWNFALL

About to Collapse

Unstable

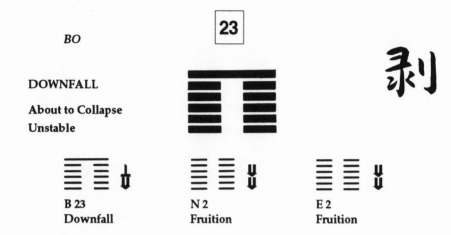

B 23
Downfall

N 2
Fruition

E 2
Fruition

When pious forces topple or lose control, your energy can easily get drained. Strengthen your supports and remain calm. This is not a time to set new goals or start new ventures. And remember, do not rely blindly on former allies or depend on "old" friends.

1. Those who support what is right are subverted, betrayed, or devastated by unfounded maliciousness and defamation.   27

2. Impending danger is personally threatening. It is perilous to remain inflexible or to count on outside help.   4

3. When you are obligated to persons whose actions are immoral or offensive, you do not have to participate. Just leave!   52

4. If things are not going well, take comfort; it won't get much worse. There is really no way to prevent this difficulty.   35

5. Take initiative to serve under or assist others. You can be a complement to help strengthen or enhance their position.   20

○ 6. Misfortune and wrongdoing will exhaust themselves or self-destruct. You are on the verge of a fresh new start.   2

FU

TURNING POINT

New Beginning
Return

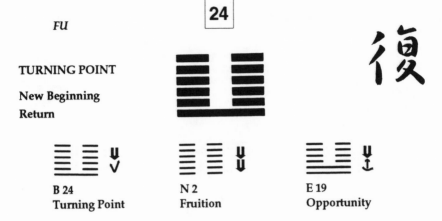

| B 24 | N 2 | E 19 |
| Turning Point | Fruition | Opportunity |

A new opportunity or change in your activities, interests, or personal growth is unfolding in a natural flowing manner. This development should be no surprise. The way is clear if you set a goal. There is no reason to hurry, so enjoy the experience.

○ 1. If digressions from what is right are not severe or last too long, you can start or return without serious problems.　　2

2. To effect a positive change, one requires perseverance, self-discipline, humility, and compatible companions.　　19

3. If one can avoid continually vacillating between the amoral, immoral, and the virtuous, things will unfold beneficially.　　36

4. Gather the strength to forgo or leave behind unvirtuous associations. Favor those with an ethical inclination.　　51

5. Face the opportunity for inner growth courageously and without rationalizations, alibis, or procrastination.　　3

6. If you miss, resist, or pass up a valuable opportunity due to stubbornness or folly, do not expect it to come again.　　27

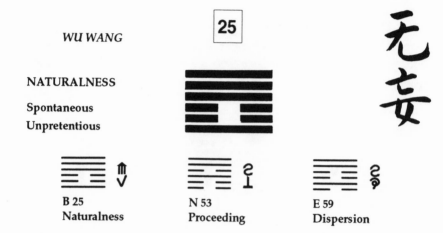

WU WANG

25

NATURALNESS

Spontaneous
Unpretentious

B 25
Naturalness

N 53
Proceeding

E 59
Dispersion

Avoid expectations or preconceptions. Respond to people and situations with genuine spontaneity. Where there are ulterior motives or new goals, misfortune will follow. Clarity of purpose and calm consideration however can generate a successful outcome.

○ 1. Heed your intuitive inclinations and first impressions spontaneously and with confidence. You will not go wrong.   12

2. If you are not preoccupied with future benefits or potential results of your present action, success is assured.   10

3. Deal correctly, especially with casual and trivial matters. Otherwise something of value will be lost or taken away.   13

4. You cannot exhaust your supply of virtue or good character. Without worrying, persist in what you know is right.   42

○ 5. Those problems that are not of your own causing should be allowed to resolve or remedy themselves.   21

6. It is best to wait patiently without desire or expectation; disastrous to instigate or provoke a particular agenda.   17

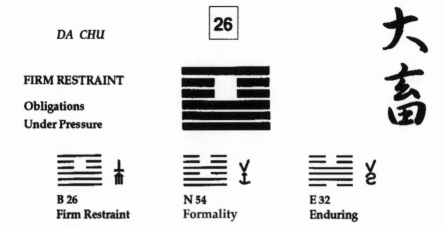

DA CHU

26

大畜

FIRM RESTRAINT

Obligations
Under Pressure

B 26
Firm Restraint

N 54
Formality

E 32
Enduring

To exercise power wisely, one must learn from history and from the experience of others. Self-restraint is nourishing. Take the time to show others your appreciation. Perseverance in new endeavors and self-reliance then hold promise for a successful outcome.

1. When your efforts to proceed are strongly thwarted, wait. Remain calm and collected until the way becomes clear.   18

2. There should not be the slightest doubt that your way is completely blocked. Do not even contemplate moving ahead.   22

3. Obstruction is removed. Refine your skills and abilities: both offensive, supportive, and defensive, preventative.   41

4. A source of future difficulty or jeopardy can be anticipated and neutralized before it manifests or becomes too late.   14

○ 5. When facing a powerful, threatening, perilous force, do not confront it head on. Block its influence indirectly.   9

○ 6. Patience is rewarded. When restraints to your mobility and efforts have ended you are free to proceed unimpeded.   11

YI

SUSTENANCE

Nourishment

Nurture

頤

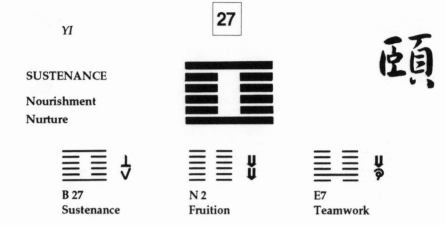

| B 27 | N 2 | E 7 |
| Sustenance | Fruition | Teamwork |

Nurture your own body, mind, and spirit. Be open and available to help others become stronger and more self-sufficient. Maintain balance and perspective. Do not advance one thing at the expense of another. Pay attention to what enters and exits your mouth.

1. It would be a sad misfortune to give up your peace or lose your self-reliance to pursue something materialistic.   23

2. Do not give up self-esteem or financial independence and put yourself at another's mercy or pursue a dream or fantasy.   41

3. It is absurd and unsound to pursue self-indulgence for its own sake. That which does not nourish will debilitate.   22

4. If you have the mind and capacity to serve others, then passionately seek out appropriate colleagues or assistants.   21

○ 5. Recognize your limitations. You need counsel and advice from someone with considerable experience and wisdom.   42

○ 6. There is nothing blocking you, even in a difficult under-taking. Remember to have your actions benefit others.   24

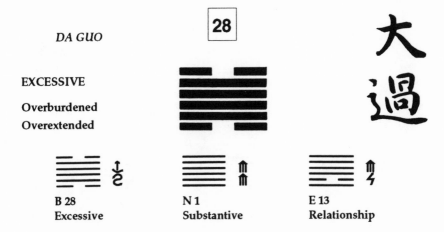

DA GUO

EXCESSIVE

Overburdened
Overextended

28

大過

B 28
Excessive

N 1
Substantive

E 13
Relationship

Too much has accumulated or is happening at once. If you become overwhelmed, then a crisis is imminent. Reinforcement is needed. Act quickly to confront such an emergency. You must be confident, steady, firm, and gentle to avert disaster and regain control.

1. Reinforce, protect, or cushion what you are doing. You cannot be too careful, especially at the beginning. 43

○ 2. The unexpected or improbable can occur when compatible but unlikely persons or elements combine in a dynamic way. 31

3. If, when experiencing stress, you go out on a limb without good support, expect things to collapse or break apart. 47

○ 4. With appropriate reinforcement or strengthening, you will avoid or overcome vulnerability. Be generously unselfish. 48

5. A somewhat unusual or surprising situation may arise that is personally rewarding but not very productive or lasting. 32

6. If you persist regardless of the consequences, you can expect misfortune. If you are selfless, you will avoid reproach. 44

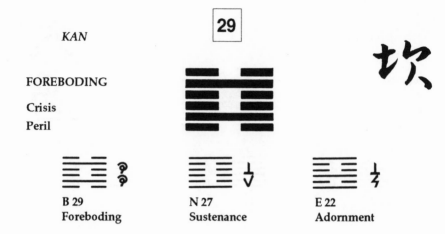

KAN

29

坎

FOREBODING

Crisis

Peril

B 29
Foreboding

N 27
Sustenance

E 22
Adornment

A current dilemma arises from a need to overcome the tension and pressure resulting from a crisis. You may have exceeded your limitations and gone too far. You can extricate yourself with sensitivity, faith, and sincerity. Let this be a lesson.

1. If you become too accustomed to danger, you will take basic precautions for granted. This can result in misfortune. 60

○ 2. When confronted by a hazardous situation, remain centered. Only then might you take on something demanding. 8

3. When difficulty lingers in every direction and there is no way out, take no action. Patiently await the right time. 48

4. Now is not a suitable time for formalities, only essentials. It is enough to have sincere intentions and be yourself. 47

○ 5. When hovering precariously on the edge of disaster, do not take any chances if you wish to enjoy a safe outcome. 7

6. Those who err are certain to become entangled and imprisoned in an inescapable web of their own making. 59

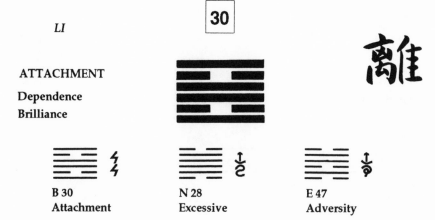

LI

30

ATTACHMENT

Dependence
Brilliance

B 30
Attachment

N 28
Excessive

E 47
Adversity

When your position or reputation are dependent on others for aid, inspiration, or creativity, it is beneficial to give them credit when and where it is due. Foster a routine or hobby that requires patience or caring. Be less erratic and more decisive.

1. Take your time. Clarity, composure, and consideration help unscramble chaos, obscuration, and confusing impressions.   56

○ 2. Peace and harmony depend on your sensitivity, perceptions, values, and even more, on how well you express them.   14

3. It is the special individual who, when facing life's brevity, can avoid despondency, depression or mindless excess.   21

4. If you eagerly try to accomplish too much, too fast, you will quickly exhaust your energy for something short-lived.   22

○ 5. Hopelessness, agony, or deep sorrow cause you to re-evaluate your life and then make profound, fundamental changes.   13

6. To correct problems and bring about permanent, substantive change, transform things at the source. Tolerate the rest.   55

XIAN

RESPONSIVE

Stimulation

Charisma

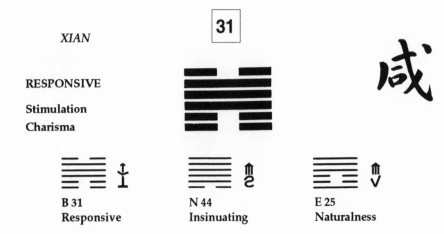

B 31	N 44	E 25
Responsive	Insinuating	Naturalness

Remain open to a new relationship, partnership, involvement, or interest. Consider the ideas and advice of others. Success is assured where you are stimulated, discerning, and supportive. Have or develop a common goal and share responsibilities equally.

1. Be sensitive and attuned to conditions as they begin to occur, but before they are evident or apparent to others.   49

2. Do not act in anticipation or expectation. Deal with situations as they arise and respond to them appropriately.   28

3. Develop restraint and self-discipline. Do not acquiesce too readily to others or give in impulsively to your desires.   45

○ 4. People will stick by you if you do not drag them into your emotional vacillations and indecision. It is exhausting.   39

○ 5. Be resolute. Free yourself from ulterior motives and societal and political manipulations and pressures.   62

6. When employing your (verbal) abilities, be mindful not to exploit others or unfairly influence or suppress them.   33

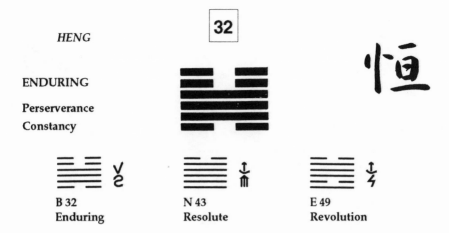

HENG

32

ENDURING

Perserverance
Constancy

恒

B 32
Enduring

N 43
Resolute

E 49
Revolution

Relationships need adaptability and commitment to last. Become resolute and strong as well as sensitive and responsive. Focus your energy into a single commitment, a serious avocation, or one specific interest. You will be amply rewarded.

1. When something is just starting, it is harmful to impose the burden of permanence on it. Do not needlessly rush things. 34

2. One's willingness to achieve something is not matched by one's commitment. Moderate objectives diminish regret. 62

3. If you allow yourself to be bounced around by external conditions you don't comprehend, you can expect to suffer. 40

4. It is not enough to try intently to do something seriously. Your effort must be correct, timely, and appropriate. 46

5. The way of accord, accommodation, or tradition is auspicious and rewarded. But do not let it obstruct your obligations. 28

6. One who is constantly under pressure, restless, or impatient is at risk and finds it difficult to be benevolent. 50

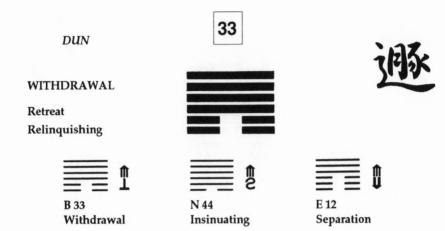

DUN

33

WITHDRAWAL

Retreat

Relinquishing

B 33
Withdrawal

N 44
Insinuating

E 12
Separation

To persist or resist in the face of a strong obstacle or a hopeless, intolerable confrontation would bring regrets. Retreating or calmly removing yourself is not only wise, but a step that creates new options. Moderate achievements then become possible.

☐ 1. You may have left a precarious situation behind you, but the peril or problem is still much too close for comfort.   13

☐ 2. It is auspicious to cling tenaciously close to those you are serving, working for, following, or learning from.   44

   3. Though your mind may be decided and your direction firmly set, expect confused associates to frustrate or delay you.   12

   4. It is advantageous to depart cordially before it becomes necessitated. Those you leave will be the real losers.   53

○ 5. By remaining totally resolute, you can depart harmoniously, elegantly, and on completely agreeable or pleasant terms.   56

   6. When you are not preoccupied with or attached to an outcome, you can depart with a clear mind and joyful assurance.   31

126

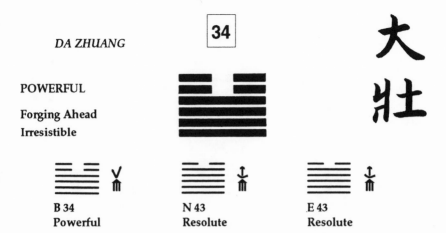

DA ZHUANG

34

大
壯

POWERFUL

Forging Ahead
Irresistible

B 34
Powerful

N 43
Resolute

E 43
Resolute

Your character, disposition, and attitude have a significant influence on others. You should not waste or abuse this responsibility. Your success is directly proportionate to how the persons you affect are benefited, or otherwise enhanced.

1. One who is unprepared or incapable should not try to achieve this. If you insist on proceeding, expect misfortune. 32

2. Your efforts can eliminate initial obstacles, so persist until the end. Do not let this success go to your head. 55

3. It is foolish to display your resources unnecessarily. Do not employ force, except with deliberation and good cause. 54

○ 4. Truly immense power is rarely apparent, and yet not much can withstand its quiet, steady, concentrated application. 11

5. When hindrances and obstacles are gone, you can abandon your intense or aggressive tendencies without losing anything. 43

6. Where you have created an impossibly difficult, restrictive situation for yourself, let matters work themselves out. 14

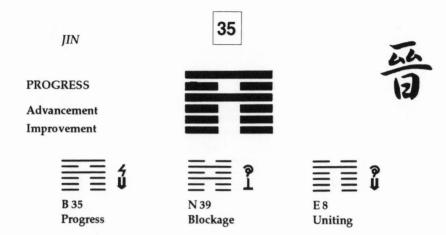

JIN

35

PROGRESS

Advancement
Improvement

B 35
Progress

N 39
Blockage

E 8
Uniting

It is possible for two incompatible persons to cooperate in a venture in which both are furthered. An astute leader should give responsibility and authority to a dynamic, energetic colleague. His or her initiative and achievement may exceed expectations.

1. Do not yield to outside pressures and thereby sacrifice what is right. It is unnecessary to impress or convince others.   21

2. It is regrettable but unavoidable when someone steps between people to prevent their relating. Remain optimistic.   64

3. In situations where you cannot achieve things alone, gladly accept and enjoy the support and encouragement of others.   56

4. When one accumulates substantial property in a questionable manner, you can be sure that nothing remains concealed.   23

○ 5. By not always pressing for the maximum possible advantage, you are assured of continued and beneficial effectiveness.   12

6. It is precarious to aggressively correct or instruct others. It may be appropriate, however, with one's own colleagues.   16

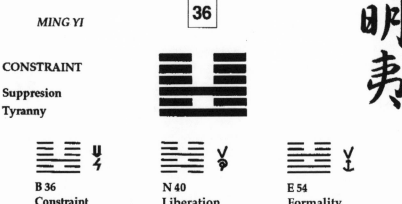

MING YI

CONSTRAINT

Suppresion
Tyranny

36

明夷

B 36
Constraint

N 40
Liberation

E 54
Formality

When antagonistic and oppressive forces govern or affect your situation, maintain a low profile. It is auspicious to appear compliant. Yield on all non-essential matters. Keep your basic principles concealed and safely uncompromised.

1. When the choice is between giving up some things you are used to or compromising your values, there is no choice. 15

○ 2. You may be effectively disabled, but not seriously. Do not get dramatic or preoccupied with this. Just help others. 11

3. You can overcome the cause of your upset or confusion by dealing with things directly when they are encountered. 24

4. An intense look at the actual condition will convince you to depart safely while it is still possible. 55

○ 5. When you are caught in a dangerous or compromising situation be strong and keep your true feelings to yourself. 63

☐ 6. Negative energy or disposition that has nothing to feed on will destroy itself. Do not provide it with food or fuel. 22

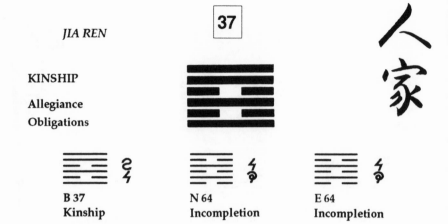

JIA REN

37

KINSHIP

Allegiance
Obligations

| B 37 | N 64 | E 64 |
| Kinship | Incompletion | Incompletion |

Meaningful and substantive relationships grow where there is honesty and commitment. Be yourself and not as you think or hope others see you. Divide responsibilities and respect each other's space. Continually examine your strengths and weaknesses.

1. Within your personal group or family, establish individual obligations and share responsibilities from the start. 53

○ 2. In serving others, be concerned with taking care of the duties you have assumed. Do not get side-tracked. 9

3. With significant latitude, restrictions and restraint are definitely desirable. Extreme laxity brings humiliation. 42

4. Great rewards come to those who maintain cohesion with their dedication, thoroughness, and sense of equitability. 13

○ 5. You will accomplish more and establish confidence by setting a good example, not by instilling fear or panic. 22

6. When it is necessary to take charge, a strong and yet agreeable personality exerts a positive influence on others. 63

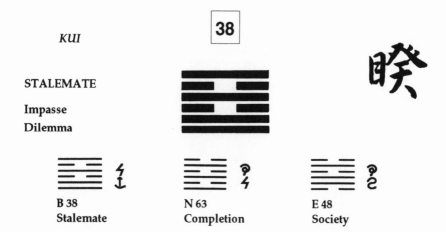

KUI

38

STALEMATE

Impasse

Dilemma

B 38
Stalemate

N 63
Completion

E 48
Society

When you are immobile, undecided, or held in check by opposing forces of either an external or internal nature, risk making a decision. It inspires confidence and gets you moving. Avoid preconceptions or partiality. Opposites will complement each other.

   1. When you are unable to overcome disharmony or difficulties, be patient. Later on, matters will set themselves right.   64

○ 2. When alienated parties desire harmony or yearn for reunion, a relaxed and indirect approach is preferable.   21

   3. One is disgraced or restrained and impeded at every turn. Hold firm. With trust and perseverance, things end well.   14

   4. Alienation arises from a fundamental difference in values or principles. Accord is reached with the help of a friend.   41

○ 5. Discover cooperation or genuine friendship by penetrating another's aloof or protective barrier with your sincerity.   10

   6. A misperception can cause you to mistakenly judge another too harshly. Relax and enjoy what can be shared.   54

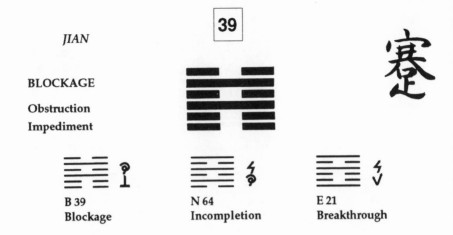

JIAN

BLOCKAGE

Obstruction
Impediment

寒

B 39
Blockage

N 64
Incompletion

E 21
Breakthrough

The obstacles are immense. It is imperative to withdraw and get good advice. Ultimately you must rely on your resources, ethics, and convictions to achieve a substantive but delayed success. This does not mean that you have to deal with this alone.

1. Hold back! Retreat or refrain from going ahead with your plans and take time to consider what is best and when.   63

2. Obligations may require you to engage difficulties directly but it is usually best to circumvent or avoid them.   48

3. Where others depend primarily on you, your responsibilities supersede any personal wish to pursue other matters.   8

4. Preserve self-restraint for awhile. Stay put, find reliable assistance, plan carefully, and approach things indirectly.   31

○ 5. Where someone is petitioned to aid a person in serious need, help must be willingly organized and effectively provided.   15

6. One who has successfully withdrawn from dealing with certain matters or affairs is still available in an emergency.   53

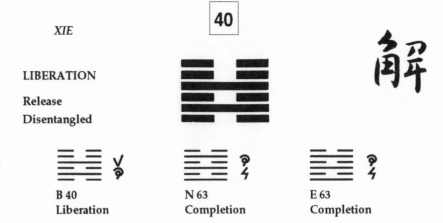

XIE

40

LIBERATION

Release
Disentangled

B 40
Liberation

N 63
Completion

E 63
Completion

The main difficulty has passed. Handle new problems as they arise and without procrastination. It is unwise to push either yourself or others. Do not be abusive or severe on those who oppose you. Remain humble. Things will return to normal shortly.

1. Once your main hurdle is behind you, no one can fault you for taking some well-deserved time to recover your energy.   54

○ 2. To overcome elusive, clever, or subtle adversaries or bad habits, develop a careful, direct, and coherent strategy.   16

3. Insecurity could lead to carelessness or overprotection in guarding your assets. This could bring about their loss.   32

4. Real friends continue to be wary and distant as long as you remain committed to persons or matters of dubious worth.   7

○ 5. People whose attachments confine and restrain you will not let go until they understand that you are really serious.   47

6. You must tenaciously eliminate all the remaining traces of obstruction that are blocking the way to resolution.   64

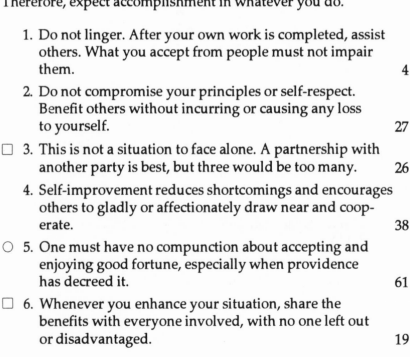

SUN

DECREASE

Reduction
Diminished

B 41
Decrease

N 24
Turning Point

E 46
Striving

When you experience loss, release, or a letting go, do not ignore it. Remain centered and free of attachment. Your objectivity and sincerity will lead to growth or benefits that far outweigh the loss. Therefore, expect accomplishment in whatever you do.

1. Do not linger. After your own work is completed, assist others. What you accept from people must not impair them.   4

2. Do not compromise your principles or self-respect. Benefit others without incurring or causing any loss to yourself.   27

☐ 3. This is not a situation to face alone. A partnership with another party is best, but three would be too many.   26

4. Self-improvement reduces shortcomings and encourages others to gladly or affectionately draw near and cooperate.   38

○ 5. One must have no compunction about accepting and enjoying good fortune, especially when providence has decreed it.   61

☐ 6. Whenever you enhance your situation, share the benefits with everyone involved, with no one left out or disadvantaged.   19

YI

INCREASE

Prospering

Enhanced

益

≡≡ ⵁ

B 42
Increase

≡≡ ⵂ

N 23
Downfall

≡≡ ⵃ

E 4
Inexperienced

See things for what they are. Change is surely for the better so take the initiative, handle it maturely, and do something about it. Consider a new venture or experience. Accentuate the positive eliminate the negative, and enjoy the benefits while they last.

☐ 1. If you experience a boost of energy or good fortune, make the best use of it generously and in a sharing manner.   20

○ 2. An open spirit and a loving heart form the foundation for naturally and deliberately enhancing one's prosperity.   61

3. Those who profit or benefit from another's misfortune are free of blame if they did not precipitate or exploit it.   37

☐ 4. Both parties stand to gain from a dispute, but an objective mediator is needed for an equitable, amiable settlement.   25

○ 5. Authentic kindness and generosity are shared for their own sake, without expecting compliments or acknowledgment.   27

6. If you pass up an opportunity to benefit persons less fortunate, you will find yourself isolated and vulnerable.   3

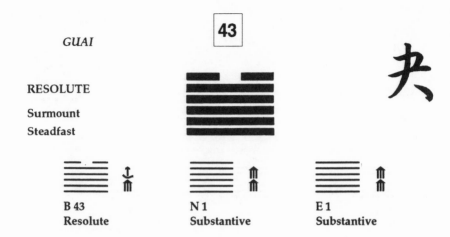

GUAI

43

RESOLUTE

Surmount
Steadfast

B 43
Resolute

N 1
Substantive

E 1
Substantive

This is an opportune time for a significant breakthrough in your growth or aspirations. Conviction and honesty, especially with yourself, will further whatever endeavor you pursue. Share the changes, remain positive, and be prepared to defend your position.

1. Calculate your resources and stay within the limits of your capability. Overambition tends to end disastrously. 28

2. By remaining composed, prepared, and vigilant you can face or encounter adversity free of panic, anxiety, or fear. 49

3. The situation is, at best, precarious. If you try to balance both sides, expect to be misunderstood and maligned. 58

4. Stubbornness results in an irrational course of action or unsound decision-making. The obstructions are avoidable. 5

○ 5. You must be constant to overcome those counter-productive patterns that undermine your life. Stay your course. 34

☐ 6. If you are a little careless before success is completely in hand, you can expect problems to recur or get worse. 1

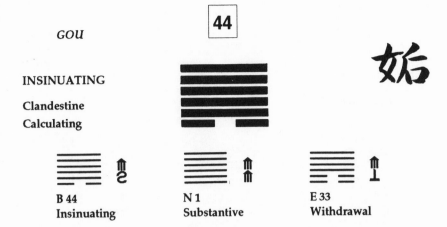

GOU

44

姤

INSINUATING

Clandestine
Calculating

B 44	N 1	E 33
Insinuating	Substantive	Withdrawal

When you believe you are in complete control, beware of concealed problems or hidden agendas. Do not become tempted, distracted or give an apparently innocent or charming person power they can use against you. Keep perspective. Things are not what they seem.

☐ 1. You will not overcome weaknesses or desires by indulging them. Surmount them before they get out of hand.　　1

○ 2. Resorting to aggression and struggle is no way to resolve matters. Try quiet influence and flexible diplomacy.　　33

3. Inner conflicts can lead to meaningful insight. You will probably be saved from disaster in spite of yourself.　　6

4. Learn to patiently put up with situations and persons you would prefer to avoid. You will benefit later from this.　　57

○ 5. Responsible persons must be tolerant and protective of those in their charge or care, and yet give them some latitude.　　50

6. One who successfully disassociates from surrounding chaos may appear disdainful but becomes immune to criticism.　　28

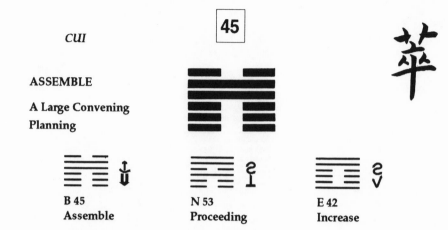

CUI

45

ASSEMBLE

A Large Convening
Planning

B 45
Assemble

N 53
Proceeding

E 42
Increase

A time of enjoyable convening is indicated. Be prepared, however, to deal reasonably with the unexpected. Advantage comes through generosity and sharing ethical or philosophical ideals. Reinforce leadership, take initiative, and do not hesitate to get advice.

1. One who extends a firm and helping hand gives confidence and assurance to those who are still unsure or undecided. 17

2. Remain thoughtful, sensitive, and open to change. Make your decisions about whom you will associate with intuitively. 47

3. Where you wish to associate with others but feel alienated, appeal boldly but sincerely to those in charge. 31

○ 4. Efforts to accomplish something will surely succeed if they are based on generosity rather than selfishness. 8

○ 5. One who is virtuous and patient will attract and transform people who are curious as well as those who are sincere. 16

6. If your motives are misjudged and efforts to reach accord are thwarted, your distress should prompt a reassessment. 12

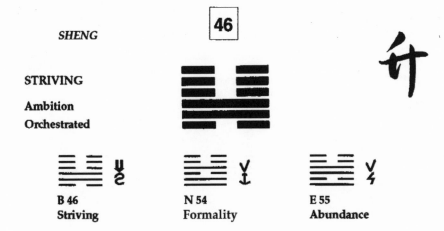

STRIVING

Ambition
Orchestrated

B 46
Striving

N 54
Formality

E 55
Abundance

Grand success is possible with a concerted step by step effort. Remain adaptable, take initiative, and do not loaf or dawdle. The progress you achieve or are responsible for will be recognized. Seek and accept advice from a worthy or meritorious individual.

☐ 1. No matter how humble or inauspicious one's position, a lofty inspiration gives him or her the impetus to advance.   11

2. Outer appearances are irrelevant, especially if a person with character and purpose makes a simple, sincere proposal.   15

3. Your efforts permit you to proceed almost too smoothly. Do not worry. The lack of obstructions is auspicious.   7

4. With personal effort you can achieve your objective and perhaps some deserved recognition, honor, or esteem.   32

○ 5. Continue in a clear, calm, steady, orderly way. Do not let your progress or the heights of success make you dizzy.   48

6. One who persists in blindly forging ahead in the dark will soon become lost and exhausted. Change your attitude.   18

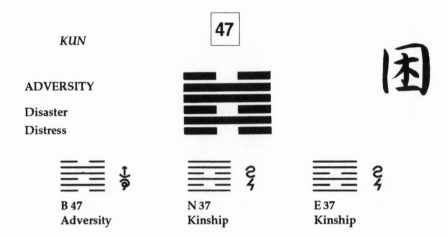

KUN

47

ADVERSITY

Disaster

Distress

困

B 47
Adversity

N 37
Kinship

E 37
Kinship

You may feel your energy and resources draining, or you may feel hemmed in. Remain buoyant. Risk being committed. Considerate actions speak louder than words. If you persevere, your problems will dissipate and you will be free of impropriety or jealousy.

1. Surrendering to misfortune intensifies disappointment and feelings of hopelessness. This attitude can be overcome.   58

○ 2. One whose life feels empty in spite of material well-being should turn within to self-reflection and contemplation.   45

3. If misfortune blinds one to common sense, even close friends will depart. This is not only sad but can be disastrous.   28

4. When one is divided and caught between conflicting forces it is difficult to do what is right. But right can prevail.   29

○ 5. It is discouraging when those who should assist or bolster you intentionally do not. Have faith, things will change.   40

6. You can readily extricate or disentangle yourself from your bonds. You are limited only by indecision or apprehension.   6

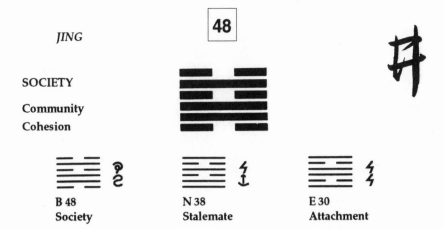

JING

SOCIETY

Community
Cohesion

B 48
Society

N 38
Stalemate

E 30
Attachment

Your actions influence others so plan carefully. Learn to give and receive openly and unconditionally. Cover your basics well: material, financial, emotional, and spiritual. Do not compromise. Cooperation and commitment keep things flowing. Avoid extremes.

1. Not many wish to be with a person who is full of self-pity or who has pathetically given up on the dignity of life.　　5

2. What good is it to have something of value and then neglect it? Beware! It will soon be lost, forgotten, or dissipated.　　39

3. It is regrettable when something of worth or someone of good character is squandered. Everyone could have benefited.　　29

4. When things are temporarily out of commission to undergo improvement or repair, benefits can be expected later.　　28

○ 5. Though resources and opportunity for growth and development abound, they are useless if they are not put to use.　　46

6. The true reservoir of knowledge, inspiration, and wisdom is available to all. Such a treasure can never be exhausted.　　57

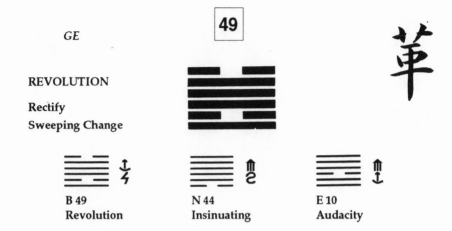

GE

49

REVOLUTION

Rectify
Sweeping Change

B 49	N 44	E 10
Revolution	Insinuating	Audacity

When you are caught in an unavoidable, drastic struggle, do not get combative or defensive. Remain clear-headed, plan ahead, and flow with conditions. Do your best and things work themselves out, although as it now appears no one would believe it possible.

1. Do not press forward to take initiative except perhaps as a last resort. Continued restraint is an absolute must. 31

2. After all peaceful and customary means are exhausted, resort to initiating a well-organized and drastic change. 43

3. Do not overreact. First rectify or remedy any inequality or imbalance. But do not hesitate to make a complete change. 17

4. Successful change requires a decisiveness based on solid principles and reflects authentic, essential necessity. 63

○ 5. Change can be enacted boldly and openly. When one is clear, decisive, and capable, the outcome is quite impressive. 55

6. Set goals that insure stability and are realistic. After major issues are resolved, one must tend to the details. 13

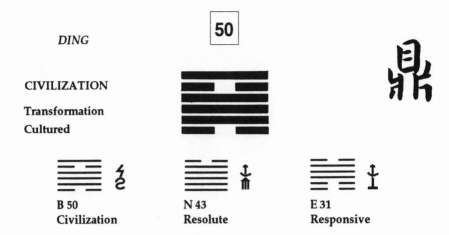

DING

50

CIVILIZATION

Transformation
Cultured

B 50
Civilization

N 43
Resolute

E 31
Responsive

Embrace an opportunity with significant responsibility. Do not dwell in the past, nor rush into the future. All actions should be mutually beneficial. Three supports provide steadiness. Humility and a sense of destiny attract success and lead to understanding.

1. Start with the basics, clearing up and cleaning out. This is a genuine opportunity to progress or achieve something.   14

2. Efforts at self-improvement might create jealousy. The more you keep this to yourself, the better off you will be.   56

3. Accept who you are and be less concerned with approval. You can accomplish something with a change in attitude.   64

4. You cannot expect to succeed if you take on more than you can handle or if you give less than your best effort.   18

○ 5. Modesty and accessibility attract cooperation, which enhances or advances your efforts. But pride will alienate you.   44

○ 6. One who exudes genuine warmth, has pure motives, clear goals, and is not easily impressed, will achieve much.   32

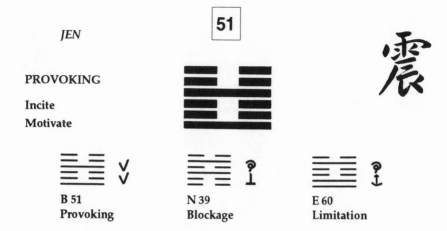

JEN

51

PROVOKING

Incite
Motivate

B 51
Provoking

N 39
Blockage

E 60
Limitation

When you are shocked, startled, or overwhelmed by persuasiveness and exuberance, remain outwardly congenial and calm and inwardly guarded and confident. The astonishment could either advance or oppose you. Use restraint, think clearly, and ride this through.

○ 1. Any initial fear or upset due to shock or surprise is easily overcome. It could even provide helpful stimulation.   16

2. Losses must not be resisted or pursued. In due time you will recover completely, so take all this philosophically.   54

3. One must respond appropriately to the jolts in life. What will overwhelm one person may inspire another.   55

4. If you become bogged down and nothing responds to your efforts, use this experience as an exercise in patience.   24

5. One who can remain centered in the midst of confusion and chaos will avoid being pummeled and suffer no loss.   17

6. If you have the capacity and clarity to recognize impending disaster, you can take the necessary steps to avert it.   21

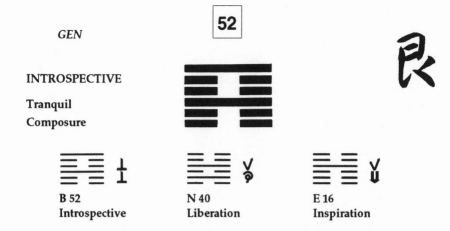

52

INTROSPECTIVE

Tranquil
Composure

B 52
Introspective

N 40
Liberation

E 16
Inspiration

Continue calmly with what you are doing. Be patient and focused, using this time for reflection and contemplation. Still your mind and quiet your heart, becoming aware of your inner self and your limitations. Avoid daydreaming, worry, and idle curiosity.

1. While adhering to your goal, resist the desire to proceed for now. The correct approach will unfold intuitively.　22

2. It is not enough to know what is right if you are not willing to liberate yourself from harmful or destructive ways.　18

3. It is unacceptable and dangerous to force something on yourself or another just because you think it will be good.　23

4. When you cannot subdue your ego completely, be content to have a limited measure of control over your mind and body.　56

5. You can avoid regret by learning to check the unkind things you might say in moments of anger or frustration.　53

○ 6. Do not be satisfied with partial or incomplete achievement, especially where inner peace or awareness are concerned.　15

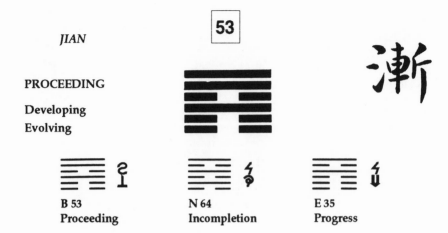

53

JIAN

漸

PROCEEDING

Developing
Evolving

B 53
Proceeding

N 64
Incompletion

E 35
Progress

Allow development to occur gradually, without delay or hurry, and free of outside influence or imposition. Focus on your goals and methods without worrying about others. Respect existing mores and customs, make firm commitments, and persist in your course.

1. Take your time, mindful of the difficulties, especially at the beginning. Do not let outright criticism deter you. 37

○ 2. Establish a solid base. This will provide you with security and enough to meet your needs. Share the excess you have. 57

3. For your own benefit and safety, do not venture too far. What is at risk may be protected or secured defensively. 20

4. In making an auspicious transition, one can find advantage in otherwise unsuitable places by being resourceful. 33

○ 5. As you approach the summit, you may find yourself let down or unjustly wronged and alone. This is resolved in due time. 52

6. It is auspicious to meet with one who has attained success or fulfillment. One's actions speak for themselves. 39

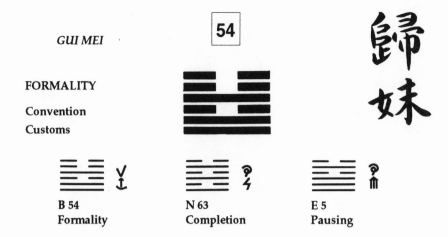

GUI MEI

54

歸妹

FORMALITY

Convention

Customs

B 54
Formality

N 63
Completion

E 5
Pausing

Enjoy this for what it is. Relationships of convenience rarely become substantive or serious. Most problems can be overcome with kindness, affection, or consideration. Pursuing this interest in spite of the obstacles can lead to difficulty and disappointment.

1. When entering a new situation, accept the existing condition and adapt it. Although limiting, it can be satisfying. 40

2. If you are committed to someone who fails to meet reasonable expectations, it benefits to continue a while longer. 51

☐ 3. You would find it worthwhile and substantially rewarding to forgo your pride and generally make the best of things. 34

4. If you hold fast to your values and withstand the pressures to compromise or settle for less, you are amply rewarded. 19

○ 5. When you are involved in a significant collaboration, you must subordinate your personal interests and desires. 58

☐ 6. If you make the effort to do something, do it well. It is meaningless to be concerned only with the external form. 38

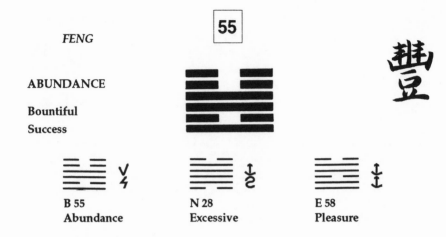

FENG

55

ABUNDANCE

Bountiful

Success

B 55
Abundance

N 28
Excessive

E 58
Pleasure

Be appreciative for what you have acquired or created. Manage your affairs or assets responsibly and decisively. Always be just and where necessary be firm. Do not overextend yourself or become selfish and greedy. Make an effort to find fulfillment within.

1. Those destined to play constructive and significant roles in each other's lives will easily spend (much) time together.   62

2. In times of drastic change, maintain a low profile. You can easily learn to recognize those who think as you do.   34

3. When worthy elements are obscured or when you are distracted by what is inferior, it is impossible to achieve anything.   51

4. You should strive to balance your abundance with wisdom. This requires desire and a moderate degree of clarity.   36

○ 5. One who is open to advice will attract many suggestions and opinions, some of which are valuable and worth accepting.   49

6. One who acquires much and yet desires to maintain complete control is overbearing, insufferable, and ends up alone.   30

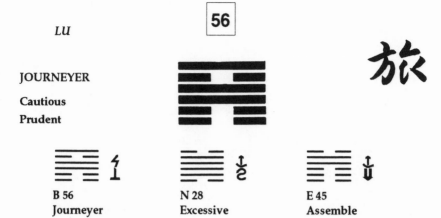

LU

JOURNEYER

Cautious
Prudent

56

旅

B 56
Journeyer

N 28
Excessive

E 45
Assemble

Like a journeyer, be respectful and continually adaptable to shifting conditions. Be honest about your plans and intentions. If you do not abuse kindness and hospitality or make distant promises and commitments, progress in minor matters is possible.

1. Outwardly, remain humble but with dignity. Do not waste your energy on trivial, foolish, or irrelevant matters. 30

2. If you are personable, unpretentious, and interested in other people, you will find them continually helpful and kind. 50

3. Be mindful that your disposition and behavior are above reproach, not indecent, vulgar, insolent, or meddlesome. 35

4. One who is self-sufficient, secure, or successful may still be dissatisfied. Question the meaning of life. 52

○ 5. Remain open and sincere. One who is capable, adaptable, and who has something to offer or share is always welcome. 33

6. One would regret allowing a time of celebration or frivolity to drift into rash behavior, incaution, or recklessness. 62

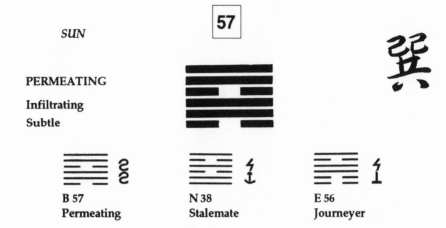

SUN

PERMEATING

Infiltrating

Subtle

B 57
Permeating

N 38
Stalemate

E 56
Journeyer

Form a clear objective. Do not be aimless. Seek a supporting role to assist a capable individual or project. Moderate your personal desires, stabilize your emotions and get some good advice. You can achieve or influence more with subtlety and flexibility.

☐ 1. Do not permit pensive or temperate manners to dissipate into indecision. Make a plan and resolutely follow through.   9

2. The most difficult adversary is the one that cannot be seen. Make a concerted effort. What is revealed can be overcome.   53

3. One can plan, try, or ponder too much. Do not try, just do! Your inaction could bring embarrassment or disgrace.   59

☐ 4. A success sufficiently sizable to fully benefit yourself and others requires opportunity, experience, and vitality.   44

○ 5. An alternative is available. Take up the challenge to make a change. Plan ahead and reflect on it afterward.   18

6. Although you may comprehend what needs to be done, consider that you may not have the energy or resources to do it.   48

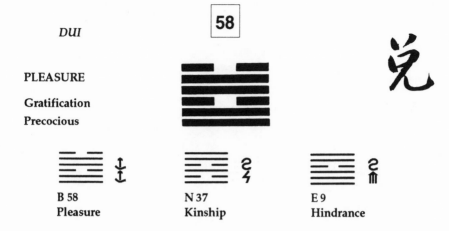

DUI

58

PLEASURE

Gratification
Precocious

兑

| B 58 | N 37 | E 9 |
| Pleasure | Kinship | Hindrance |

Proceed confidently, with calmness, strength, and integrity. You can make others feel good, but do not let joy deteriorate into wanton sensuality or self-gratification. Cheerful sharing and support can help others temporarily forget pressing difficulties.

1. Gladly accept what you have, without further expectation. This will be liberating and bring its own fulfillment.   47

○ 2. A situation or companion may be most agreeable but you would regret abandoning yourself to indiscriminate enjoyment.   17

☐ 3. Where there are no feelings of inner joy or warmth, one may become lost in a spiral of constant gratification.   43

4. Measured pleasure reflects desire and culminates in turmoil. Real joy is spontaneous. Aspire to higher pleasure.   60

○ 5. Compassion has its place. Do not be enticed or compromised into associating with disruptive or dishonorable persons.   54

☐ 6. Sensual gratification may be covering up low self-esteem and insecurity. Both conditions need attention and assurance.   10

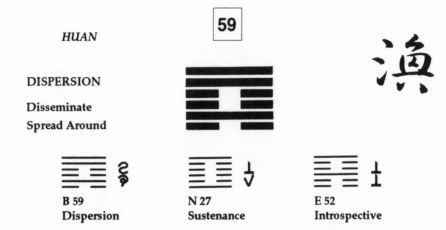

HUAN

DISPERSION

Disseminate
Spread Around

B 59	N 27	E 52
Dispersion	Sustenance	Introspective

Eliminate emotional burdens, physical blockages, and bad habits. They weigh you down. Open your heart, integrate or harmonize your various qualities, and persist optimistically. Your difficulties will soon pass and you can venture freely or join with others.

1. Open communication can resolve those conditions that lead to estrangement, alienation, or dissolution. 61

☐ 2. If people begin to avoid you, stay affable, self-assured, and see the best in them. Do not become hostile or defensive. 20

3. Becoming totally concentrated on a difficult challenge helps you overcome your ego, which alienates you from others. 57

☐ 4. Achieve significant things by looking beyond your personal interests or group associations to a broader perspective. 6

5. When things are at an impasse, a spark of inspiration can provide the necessary boost to get them moving again. 4

○ 6. One who has presence of mind can be instrumental in helping extricate others from difficulty or avoid it completely. 29

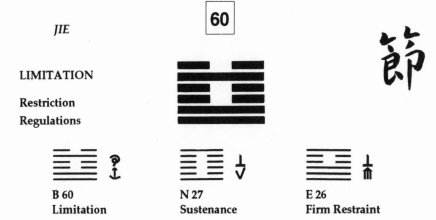

JIE

LIMITATION

Restriction
Regulations

60

節

B 60
Limitation

N 27
Sustenance

E 26
Firm Restraint

You cannot be all things to all people. Be honest with yourself; do not overburden yourself. Reasonable self-restraint is imperative. Remain creative, inquisitive, and unpretentious, limiting risky temptations and protecting what is important.

1. Be aware of personal limitations. Should you venture forth in a delicate situation, combine strength and discretion.   29

2. After a time, hesitation is no longer a function of wisdom but of insecurity. A missed opportunity is detrimental.   3

3. If you lose yourself in excess or gratification, you must assume personal responsibility for the outcome.   5

4. Setting sensible and natural limitations will not only avoid stress and conflict, but also help in conserving energy.   58

○ 5. Demanding more of yourself and less of others will prevent resistance and set an example that people will follow.   19

6. Severe or harsh restraints may be employed in an emergency. If prolonged unnecessarily, they would prove injurious.   61

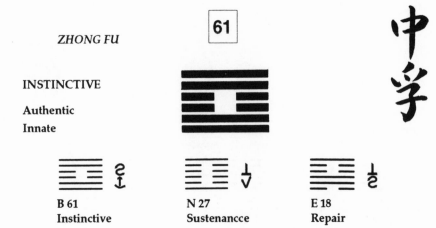

ZHONG FU

INSTINCTIVE

Authentic
Innate

61

中孚

B 61
Instinctive

N 27
Sustenancce

E 18
Repair

An open mind and a generous heart will endear you to others, so uphold the trust they place in you. Remain patient and candid and avoid rash decisions or prejudging. Engage people at their own level or capacity. Right action is mutually beneficial.

1. If you suppress or conceal things, it will upset your peace of mind and freedom. Do not depend on others for support.   59

2. A genuine offer to share should be responded to favorably. The less it concerns one's self, the greater the response.   42

☐ 3. It is difficult to share the commitment of love or affection and still remain emotionally independent and centered.   9

☐ 4. Do not let personal interests or even dear friends deter you from pursuing lofty motives, goals, or aspirations.   10

○ 5. A resolute, determined person can harmoniously integrate divergent elements into a unified, cohesive entity.   41

6. Achievement requires effort and sacrifice. Words alone can be inspiring, but in excess are diverting, not fulfilling.   60

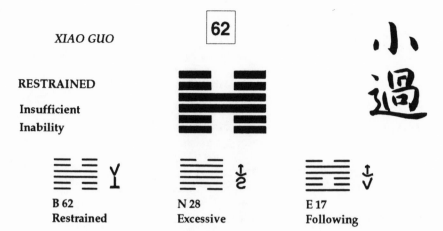

XIAO GUO

RESTRAINED

Insufficient

Inability

B 62	N 28	E 17
Restrained	**Excessive**	**Following**

When your efforts seem thwarted, keep excesses small and on the safe side. Compromise only with non-essentials and expect difficulty if you forge ahead. "Less and near" are better than "more and far." Moderate endeavors will achieve modest success.

1. If you act prematurely, before you are ready, do so only as a last resort. A conventional approach is recommended. 55

2. Take the initiative to do what you believe is right, but have a valid reason. Do not persist if you confront resistance. 32

3. Self-assurance must not interfere with your taking normal precautions. Anticipate subtle difficulty from the flank. 16

4. Do not proceed on your own initiative. You must exercise strength of character in order to restrain yourself. 15

○ 5. With quiet patience, you will find or furnish a missing link. Until then, nothing of value can be accomplished. 31

6. One who has not acquired authority will suffer misfortune if he or she tries too hard to achieve or avoid something. 56

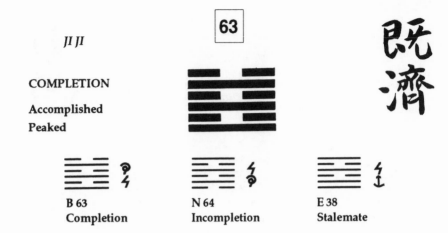

JI JI

COMPLETION

Accomplished
Peaked

63

B 63
Completion

N 64
Incompletion

E 38
Stalemate

Affairs may appear to be in order and the outcome promising, but you should realize that this situation is unpredictable, unstable, and even volatile. Modest ambitions can be successful but nothing ahead is sure, safe, or easy. Plan carefully for any eventuality.

1. If you allow yourself to get carried away, you will lose your better judgment but suffer only a minor setback. 39

○ 2. Should you lose someone's confidence or trust, do not try to prove yourself. Quietly continue striving to do your best. 5

3. Only after successfully overcoming substantial, conspicuous difficulties can smaller ones be methodically dealt with. 3

4. Never lose sight of apparently insignificant problems. When people feel confident, they unwisely tend to ignore them. 49

5. Sincere generosity comes from the heart, not from the head or the pocket. Express real feelings, not pretensions. 36

6. One who becomes absorbed in looking back to feel good about one's present progress will surely provoke difficulty. 37

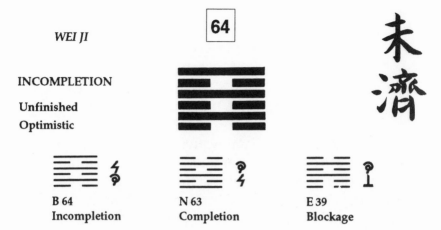

WEI JI

64

INCOMPLETION

Unfinished
Optimistic

B 64
Incompletion

N 63
Completion

E 39
Blockage

Do not rush ahead unprepared. Keep up your defenses and proceed confidently. Good judgment, constancy, effort, and ability will neutralize opposing elements and carry you toward a promising conclusion. Opportunities for resolution will present themselves.

1. When the condition is one of general confusion, wait. Decent progress can be made only when you are well prepared. 38

2. Work diligently on your character and restrain yourself from making a deliberate effort toward tangible progress. 35

3. Do not overextend yourself. If you are not quite ready when an opportunity arises, another will present itself later. 50

4. When arriving at a place of potentially significant change, energy, diligence, and strenuous effort are required. 4

○ 5. It is worthwhile to persist in your endeavor. The experience of accomplishment or impending renewal abides everywhere. 6·

6. When you have sufficient cause to celebrate, be careful not to lose your head, your common sense, or your dignity. 40

Decision-Making and Problem-Solving Without Divination

This section introduces an innovative and practical approach to using the *I Ching* for personal decision-making and problem solving. When you use this method you need to evaluate the situation at hand or the relationship under consideration, and choose the two trigrams that correlate best to the two main conditions or two primary parties. This provides a way of converting the *I Ching* system so that you can characterize a difficulty, dilemma, or some uncertainty with a pair of trigrams. You then combine the two trigrams to form a hexagram , which is used as the basis for depicting the situation within the context and framework of the *I Ching*.

This process provides a way of evaluating and analyzing situations based on traditional *I Ching* principles but without the divination. You can frame confusing or complex conditions into simpler, more manageable ones, and this makes it possible to understand problems and make insightful decisions. It is a practical and empowering way to deal with uncertainty in your personal, professional, and social life.

Whether you are new to the *I Ching* or already familiar with this ancient text and use it occasionally for divination or personal reflection, you will find this new application can be a useful supplement or alternative to divination. It can deepen your perception and broaden your understanding and experience.

The method examines situations according to their two primary components, which are characterized according to the attributes of the eight trigrams. The "situation at hand" is converted into a pair of trigrams and expressed as a hexagram. This process combines your intellect with your intuition and integrates your judgment with your natural discernment and insight. This is an innovative way to examine complex problems, to make critical choices or tough judgment calls, and resolve difficult issues.

Five Basic Conditions
for Correlating Hexagrams to Situations

The five most manageable and productive conditions that can be used to establish correlation between a hexagram and a situation and to confirm a proposed relationship between a hexagram and a situation are: 1) the hexagram name; 2) the hexagram text; 3) the trigrams, including their qualities, traditional three-line symbols, and new symbols; 4) the hexagram lines, including the interaction between the two main trigrams using the new symbols; and 5) the opposite hexagram. Figure 17 identifies each of the eight trigrams by its name, main attribute, traditional trigram symbol, and the new graphic symbol that I designed to depict the character and direction of its motion and the nature of its energy.

| Heaven | Ocean | Flame | Thunder | Wind | River | Mountain | Earth |
| creative | joyful | clinging | arousing | gentle | abysmal | still | receptive |

Figure 17. The eight trigrams with traditional and new symbols.

The name. In this book I represent each hexagram with three names or terms. These are not translations of the Chinese character(s), but are words chosen to convey the intended meaning of the hexagram as a context. The three terms provide a broader notion of each hexagram's topic or subject and the kind of situations it covers or represents.

It is important to keep two things in mind. First, the theme of each hexagram covers a large conceptual area in which the names act together to embrace, encompass, or embody. Second, the hexagram names represent all aspects of their meaning, positive and negative, constructive and destructive, helpful and detrimental. For example, hexagram 34 has the name "Power." This covers a spectrum of ideas related to power, such as: obtaining power; keeping power; letting go of power; managing power; confronting power; overcoming power; the power to uplift or diminish; personal power; organizational power; group power; and nature's power. It covers many things that are inherently neither good or bad.

The text. Each hexagram has a brief text that presents an overview of the hexagram and provides insight into its meaning and principles. The words and ideas of the text usually suggest other key factors and important values related to the hexagram theme. For example, the text for hexagram 44 Insinuating reads "when you believe you are in complete control ... ." This provides a clue to one group of conditions covered by the hexagram. If a situation relates to an issue of control, this hexagram would be a perfect candidate. If control is not a factor, this might not be an appropriate hexagram. However, if everything else about the hexagram seems right except for the issue of "control," you might want to consider that this particular form of control is very subtle, or else inherent but not yet apparent. By anticipating the control you are better prepared to deal with it.

The trigrams. These are used for selecting hexagrams and for confirming the accuracy or relevance of the hexagram you select. When the trigrams clearly relate to the situation, they are confirming. The symbols provide a layer of nonverbal meaning that can be helpful for understanding the character, energy, movement, and direction of the trigrams.

The hexagram symbol. The traditional six-line hexagram symbol is a graphic embodiment of the hexagram's meaning, informed in part by the lower and upper trigrams. The two "new" trigram symbols provide another interpretive dimension that communicates meaning at both the intuitive and intellectual or conscious level. Those who can relate to symbols will find them a very helpful and valuable asset. They become easier to interpret when you have studied or practiced the *I Ching* for a short while.

The opposite hexagram. The Opposite hexagram is formed by reversing all six hexagram lines from yang to yin and yin to yang. It represents everything that the "given" hexagram is not and can't be and doesn't include. This is useful because it is often easier to know things by "what they are not" than by "what they are." In this way the Opposite can bring additional clarity of meaning to what a hexagram is dealing with or represents.

DEPICTING RELATIONSHIPS AND SITUATIONS WITH TRIGRAMS

This is a good method for evaluating and representing a wide range of situations, and especially useful for understanding or explaining relationships between two primary parties. It is useful for two persons, for two groups, for an individual and a group, or for a person (or group) and something else, such as a problem or challenge. The important thing when correlating someone or something to a trigram is context.

Each party or element is correlated to the trigram that most closely approximates its character "in the context of the situation at hand." Once two trigrams have been identified, there are two ways to combine them: one with A below B, and the other with B below A (unless they are the same trigram). You need to determine which one best expresses the nature of the relationship, the situation, the problem, or the decision you need to make.

1. SELECTING TRIGRAMS AND FORMING A HEXAGRAM

The process of selecting a trigram for each party takes a little practice but it is not overly difficult since each trigram has a distinct personality. Two or three trigrams often share some characteristics, but they differ in the degree or manner the characteristics are expressed. A basic familiarity with the eight trigram types will enable you to identify which one best characterizes a particular person or group "within the context of the relationship" fairly easily and accurately.

If one of the parties seems to correlate almost equally to two trigrams, you will have to resolve the choice by comparing the hexagrams produced with both alternatives. For example, if one party is communicative, quick, bright, and engaging, it may not be easy to decide between Thunder ☳ and Flame ☲. If the other party is very set in its ways, yet helpful, and kind, but trying to decide what is best for others, it may well be the Mountain ☶. First form all four hexagrams: Flame below Mountain, Mountain below Flame, Thunder below Mountain, and Mountain below Thunder.

22 Adornment	56 Journeyer	27 Sustenance	62 Restrained

Figure 18. Resolving an undecided trigram by comparing hexagrams.

In most cases the hexagram names and the text will usually help you determine which one most closely represents the relationship in question. When two hexagrams are formed by the same pair of trigrams, they will represent very different conditions. For example, 22 Adornment draws attention, while 56 Journeyer avoids drawing attention; 27 Sustenance is open, nourishing, and giving, while 62 Restrained is more closed, and has narrow or limited contact. The question of which one to choose is not usually difficult.

By selecting a hexagram you can confirm the undecided trigram and then identify relative positions of the two trigrams (which is below). The hexagram then becomes the basis for effecting a constructive change.

2. CREATING A CHANGE

The six lines of each hexagram indicate the six directions or paths the relationship or situation can take. By changing one of the six lines from yang to yin or yin to yang you change one of the trigrams. This reflects a change in the basic conditions of the relationship (between trigrams), and defines a new hexagram context. The task is to choose one of the six options as the best opportunity, path, or direction of change for the relationship or situation "at this particular time."

In defining a relationship, there are two things that determine if the new hexagram condition is obtained or achieved. First, the party whose trigram has changed must take the necessary steps to bring about the change as described by the new trigram. Second, the two parties must interact constructively or positively to activate or realize the hexagram condition. This is a form of proactive change rather than passive or accepted change.

For example, if you were to describe a relationship with hexagram 27 Sustenance, which is Thunder below Mountain, the six change hexagrams from bottom to top are: 23 Downfall, 41 Decrease, 22 Adornment, 21 Breakthrough, 42 Increase, and 24 Return. The choice depends on the situation.

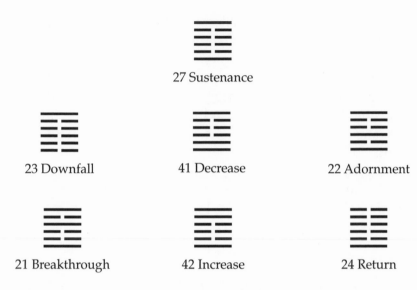

27 Sustenance

23 Downfall   41 Decrease   22 Adornment

21 Breakthrough   42 Increase   24 Return

Figure 19. The six change hexagrams for hexagram 27 Sustenance.

If you decide that the best choice is 21 Breakthrough, the upper trigram has to change from Mountain ☶ to Flame ☲. This indicates that an inert, inactive, reserved party that likes to give advice, has to start moving or warming up, and perhaps become a little more (inter-)dependent in some way. If 42 Increase is also considered an option, it requires a change of Mountain to Wind ☴. This means becoming more gentle, active, attentive to detail, and capable of managing. This explanation is intentionally oversimplified.

Figure 20 shows the relationship of each trigram to the three trigrams with two common lines. The letters indicate which line is different: "B" for bottom, "M" for middle, and "T" for top. With a change in the bottom line, the trigram River ☵ becomes Ocean ☱; with a change in the top line it becomes Wind ☴; and with a change in the middle line it becomes Earth ☷. For Thunder ☳, a change in the middle line leads to Ocean ☱; in the top line to Flame ☲; and in the bottom line to Earth ☷.

	Heaven	Lake	Fire	Thunder	Wind	Water	Mountain	Earth
Heaven		T	M		B			
Ocean	T			M		B		
Flame	M			T			B	
Thunder		M	T					B
Wind	B					T	M	
River		B			T			M
Mountain			B		M			T
Earth				B		M	T	

Figure 20. Trigrams with two common lines, indicating
which line is different: T is the top line different;
M the middle line; and B the bottom line.

3. RELATIONSHIP OF EACH TRIGRAM TO TRIGRAMS WITH TWO COMMON LINES

When you have a hexagram and then define a new hexagram by changing one line, you change one of the trigrams. This means the party or condition depicted by that trigram has to change to fit the new trigram description in order for new hexagram condition to take effect. A concerted effort may be required to accomplish or realize the objective or outcome represented by the change hexagram.

4. AN EXAMPLE OF DEPICTION

This example illustrates a way to use trigrams to represent a relationship or situation with a hexagram, and then select the path or direction you would like to take it or have it proceed. Each hexagram line is a path of change to a change hexagram, and all change necessarily starts through one of these six gates.

The six change hexagrams all have five lines in common with the starting hexagram, which means the hexagram symbols have maximum similarity or commonality.

Once you have a starting hexagram you need to choose a change hexagram as your first step in the process of changing a present relationship or situation to the one you envision or eventually want to have. This choice should be made with considerable care, with thought given to the trigram that changes and consideration given to the implications that will be created for both parties.

5. A HYPOTHETICAL RELATIONSHIP OR SITUATION

This example depicts a relationship between two persons. Kris, who is assertive, flexible, and somewhat remote; and Pat, who is independent and thinks Kris's behavior is uncaring and disinterested. In reality, Kris is very interested but preoccupied with their project, and wants to work with Pat to create a new opportunity and achieve a common goal. Kris's profile might be explained by the trigram River ☵ , which is mysterious and unfathomable. Pat is usually highly self-motivated, outgoing, independent, communicative, enthusiastic, and energetic. This behavior relates closely with the trigram Thunder ☳ . River and Thunder form two hexagrams: 3 ䷂ Initial Difficulty, with Thunder below; and 40 ䷧ Liberation, with River below. You need to determine which one best characterizes the relationship. Perhaps the hexagram name will be enough to help you make a decision. Or you may want to give more consideration to the trigram interactions. Try using the new trigram symbols to see how two trigrams interact with each other.

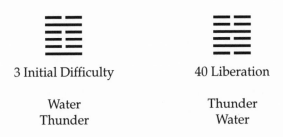

3 Initial Difficulty   40 Liberation

Water   Thunder
Thunder   Water

Figure 21. The two hexagrams composed of River and Thunder.

In 3 Initial Difficulty, Thunder is below and forging up, while River is above and flowing down. They become entangled or get caught up in each other and can spend considerable time and effort trying to get disentangled. This is not so much a condition of conflict, but one of chaos or confusion arising from uncertainty about where to go, what to do, how to do it, how to agree on matters, or how to resolve things.

In 40 Liberation, River is below and flowing down, while Thunder is above, rising upward. Here the two trigrams are becoming disentangled. This enables them to work together without getting in each other's way or to part company and go their separate ways. If you have chosen the trigrams carefully, one of these hexagrams will accurately depict or represent the relationship, or provide insight into the nature of the situation. It is unlikely that both hexagrams will be equally relevant.

6. Making choices and planning a change

I arbitrarily chose 40 Liberation, because the parties are not entangled with each other and because there is a sense of distance or remoteness between them. They could choose to cooperate or go their own separate ways. If this hexagram condition persists, the relationship could proceed smoothly as long as both parties have separate spheres of activity or responsibility that don't overlap or interfere, and as long as each manages their obligations and carries their own weight.

If the parties get along well but are not satisfied with the relationship, they should define where to take it. One way to create direction is by choosing one of the six change hexagrams for 40 ☰☰ Liberation. From bottom to top they are: 54 Formality, 16 Inspiration, 32 Enduring, 7 Teamwork, 47 Adversity, and 64 Incompletion. A quick reading of the six texts suggests several positive directions to take the relationship.

Only one hexagram appears to be problematic, 47 Adversity. When Thunder ☰☰ changes to Ocean ☰☰, it may become a little too playful, audacious, or irresponsible and get into trouble. River below Ocean is a symbol of the Ocean becoming drained, which is a form or an expression of adversity.

If you think it would be best to change from 40 Liberation to 7 ☰☰ Teamwork, the upper trigram has to change from Thunder ☰☰ to Earth ☰☰. This means Pat needs to become more collaborative (at least temporarily) by developing or nourishing characteristics associated with Earth. If this is done it will change the relationship to one of Teamwork.

If you want the relationship to be a lasting one, then select hexagram 32 Enduring. Kris, in the lower trigram position, needs to change from River ☰☰ to Wind ☰☰. This means moving beyond the familiar constraints and boundaries that guide and contain flowing River. Wind, which is generally uncomfortable with unpredictability, compensates by trying to create an ordered environment and more semblance of structure.

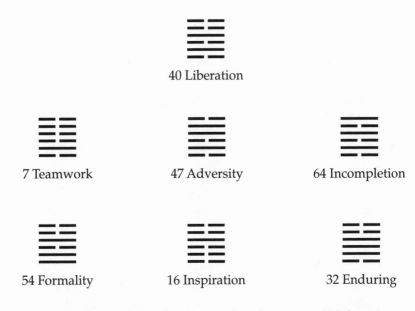

Figure 22. The six change hexagrams for a hexagram 40 Liberation.

7. DEPICTING CHANGE IN A PARTNER'S BEHAVIOR

Let's say you have accurately characterized the relationship between Kris and Pat with hexagram 40 Liberation. Some time later, Pat unexpectedly and uncharacteristically becomes dependent on Kris. This creates a dilemma or problem because Kris counts on Pat to take initiative and act or work independently. The following procedure is helpful in addressing this kind of situation:

a) Change the trigram profile for Pat so that it accurately corresponds to the behavior,

b) Consider whether Pat's trigram is still above or if the trigram changes positions,

c) Identify the new hexagram,

d) Identify the six change hexagrams and consider which one offers the best avenue for a positive development or constructive change under the present circumstances.

The key factor describing the change in Pat is "dependence," an attribute most commonly related to the trigram Flame ☲, which needs fuel and oxygen to burn. If this assessment is accurate, Pat's profile changes from Thunder to Flame. The profile for Kris is River ☵, whose lines are the exact opposite of Flame, which could explain why Kris experiences or perceives a problem. The two hexagrams formed by Flame and River are: 63 ䷾ Completion, with Flame below; and 64 ䷿ Incompletion, with River below.

Completion indicates a state of achievement, accomplishment, or "the end." When things reach a state of completion there can be a tendency to want to maintain the feeling of success or accomplishment, because completion means "end" and it is inevitably followed by a decline or a complete change.

Incompletion can indicate the possibility of accomplishment and a cause for optimism; or feeling frustrated, sad, or disheartened from realizing that one's effort might fail to achieve the goal. The question is to determine which of the two hexagrams best describes the situation or predicament, and has the change hexagram that presents the best chance for a resolution.

You can determine whether the relationship has reached a state of completion or whether it is in a process of becoming completed. Since Kris and Pat agree that they still want the relationship to move forward and accomplish something, it seems that hexagram 64 Incompletion is the more accurate choice. It is also one of the change hexagrams for 40 Liberation, which means it is conceptually closer to their starting condition because Kris's River trigram or profile remains in the lower positions. This should make Incompletion easier to deal with than Completion.

Using the new trigram symbols you can see that when River is below Flame, the trigrams move away from each other and do not integrate their energies or resources. This could explain why they can't achieve the goal. If they take initiative and do something, then they can get things done.

8. REDEFINING A RELATIONSHIP AND GIVING IT DIRECTION

The direction you take depends on the alternatives available. In this example, 64 Incompletion is the condition from which change begins. The six change hexagrams are: 38 Stalemate, 35 Progress, 50 Civilization, 4 Inexperienced, 6 Conflict, and 40 Liberation. The last is the starting hexagram. This may be a desirable outcome but is an unlikely one at this time.

There are three factors that determine which change hexagram to select. One is how well the new hexagram defines a viable opportunity, direction, or outcome. The second is whether the party that has to change its trigram profile can actually manage to do it. The third is how the change will impact the other party or affect the relationship. A quick reading of the change hexagrams suggests that 35 and 50 should be given priority.

Hexagram 35 ☷☲ Progress, requires Kris to change from River to Earth. River is like a river, active within its bounds, self-motivated, assertive, directed, and competitive. Earth has a nurturing character and is passive, yielding, and accepting. This change might be hard for Kris to accept and even harder to bring about. It might be also unacceptable to Kris because it means giving control, direction, and management over to Pat, and given Pat's dependence, that might not be desirable for the partnership.

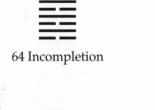

64 Incompletion

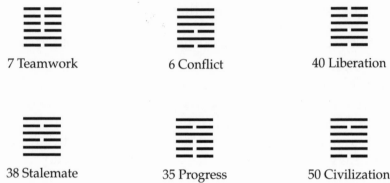

7 Teamwork   6 Conflict   40 Liberation

38 Stalemate   35 Progress   50 Civilization

Figure 23. The six change hexagrams for a hexagram 64 Incompletion.

Hexagram 50 ☴ Civilization, requires Kris to change from River to Wind, which is more structured and accountable. The text for this hexagram says, "Those who take responsibility, retain their humility, don't rush ahead, and create a mutually beneficial opportunity, can expect their actions to attract success." Kris will have to be totally committed in order to make the change from River, which is bold and daring to Wind, which is controlled and planning. This hexagram doesn't eliminate Pat's dependence but it gives Kris the ability to manage Pat's Flame by controlling how hot it burns.

Under certain conditions the parties might want to revisit 4 ☵ Inexperienced, as an alternative. In this hexagram, Kris maintains the River trigram for a profile and remains below. Pat is required to shift from Flame, which can be volatile and changeable, to Mountain, which is stable and confident. This is a difficult but not overwhelming challenge. The bottom line of the trigram changes from yang to yin. This indicates a move from being active and self-oriented to stability and consideration for the interests of others; or else defining self-interest in terms of (or within) the collective interest.

The context of hexagram 4 deals with the limitations and shortcomings that come from inexperience and ignorance, and a way out or forward as a result of seeking advice, coaching, consulting, education, information, or training. Since the predicament has arisen due to Pat's sudden dependency, this could be a viable interim solution. In the meantime, Kris will have to take the initiative until things can be resolved.

9. EXPANDED DEPICTION WHEN BOTH PARTIES CHANGE

There are many situations that would benefit by both parties changing their trigram profiles. This means that each party must be willing to change to one of the three available trigrams (see Figure 20), and be capable of making the change in character or behavior in a timely way. It also means both parties should be comfortable working with the new trigrams, as well as the hexagram conditions produced by the two changes.

Depiction differs from divination in that changing lines can be changed in any order. In this example there are two changing lines, two changing trigrams, and therefore two choices for a change or transitional hexagram; one if Kris changes first and the other if Pat changes first. It is unrealistic to expect that both parties will effect their change simultaneously. When using this model, it is best if the parties decide which transitional hexagram works best for them or their objective, and then negotiate or plan on how to proceed or act to bring it about or make it happen.

The examples in Figure 24 use a diamond-shaped hexagram arrangement template to illustrate the transitional hexagram choices in a two-party change. In "A," Kris changes from River to Earth, and Pat changes from Flame to Mountain. If Kris changes first it defines Progress; if Pat changes first it defines Inexperience. These trigrams have a concurrent lack of synchronicity or mutual support, which leads to hexagram 23 Downfall, regardless of which party changes first.

If Kris changes form River to Wind, the boundaries are removed or dissolved by becoming more organized, structured, and responsible. The result is Civilization, which is more compatible with Inexperience because the two changes lead to 18 Repair, which creates the context or environment for the parties to set things right.

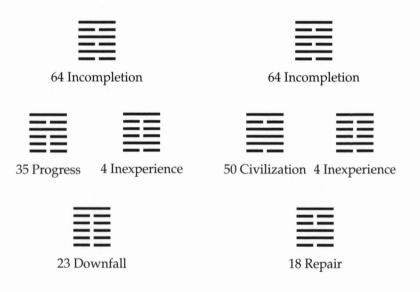

64 Incompletion   64 Incompletion

35 Progress   4 Inexperience   50 Civilization 4 Inexperience

23 Downfall   18 Repair

Figure 24. Two examples of both parties changing, starting with hexagram 64 Incompletion. The middle hexagrams are transitional options in each example.

When both parties are required to change, it is usually more difficult to achieve and coordinate than when only one party changes. The transitional options for each example are shown by the middle two hexagrams in Figure 24. The left transitions in both examples (35 and 50) reflect a change in the lower trigram (Kris); the right transitions in the examples (both 4) reflect a change in the upper trigram (Pat). Keep in mind that when there are two (or more) changes, the change usually occurs sequentially rather than simultaneously. This means one party will accomplish their change first, establishing their change hexagram as the transitional hexagram. The parties have to be prepared to deal with either transitional hexagram condition because they don't know which one will actually occur first unless they agree on one beforehand.

If this is not planned for and planned well, it could result in a transitional condition that is undesirable, counterproductive, or difficult for the parties to deal with, even when they have agreed on the outcome or ending hexagram. It can sometime mean that the first party to effect a change has to have trust and confidence that the other party will also change. This can mean giving the other party some support or assistance.

10. A REVIEW OF DEPICTION

With Depiction you define relationships or situations with two trigrams and then form a hexagram that serves as a context for your problem or decision. You then identify the change hexagram that offers the best direction or opportunity for resolution. The two keys to using Depiction effectively are: 1) to make an accurate assessment of the characteristics of the two primary parties or elements; and 2) to identify the trigram that relates best to each.

You then identify the hexagram that best describes or correlates to the situation or relationship. The hexagram becomes the starting point for initiating change. Examine the six change hexagrams and choose one as the first step in your decision process. You can also consider the benefits of both parties changing their basic trigram profile, in which case it is important to evaluate the change hexagram and the two possibilities for the transitional hexagram.

Creative and constructive change starts from the premise that the best way to deal with things is "as they are" rather than "as they could be." With a little practice you will quickly be able to use the *I Ching* for decision-making and problem-solving without divination.

GLOSSARY OF TERMS AND NAMES

Duke Zhou
: son of King Wen, d. 1094 B.C, author of the texts for the six lines of each hexagram.

Evolution
: the natural sequence of hexagrams in change. The top line moves to the bottom position and changes from yang to yin or vice versa.

existencing
: the idea representation of *being* as *becoming*, of life as an ongoing process or continuum.

Fu Xi
: a.k.a. Bao Xi, *ca.* 4000 B.C., the legendary father of Chinese culture and originator of the *I Ching* system.

Gua/gua
: the term for both hexagram and trigram. In this book, "*Gua*" is used to denote hexagram, while "*gua*" with a lower case "g" denotes trigram.

hexagram
: the six-line figures that make up the *I Ching.*

King Wen
: 1171–1122 B.C., author of the I Ching and founder of the Zhou Dynasty (pronounced *Jo*).

metaconscious
: see Note #1.

nucleus
: the four central lines of a hexagram, which recombine to form another hexagram defining the inner character of the original hexagram.

pinyin
: the standard modern romanization of Chinese words which replaced the earlier Wade system.

semiotic
: signs and symbols; the use of one symbol or word to represent another; the science of symbols.

tai ji
: in Wade spelling, *t'ai chi,* "supreme ultimate," the totality of the universe itself; this is represented by the familiar black and white circular figure on p. 20.

Ten Wings
: the commentaries to the *I Ching* written by senior students of Confucius (551–478 B.C.) in the century following his death.

Transition
: an interim stage that occurs when a hexagram changes into a second hexagram that has two or more lines different from the original hexagram.

Yijing
: this is the *pinyin* for *I Ching;* written about 1152 B.C. and originally titled *Zhou Yi* or *Zhou Changes. Yi* means change or transformation, and *jing* may be translated as Classic.

Notes

1. Metaconscious: this term has been chosen to express what the great yogi Sri Aurobindo referred to as the "all knowing" part of the self attuned to universal knowledge and consciousness. The psychologist Carl Jung, who wrote the foreword to Richard Wilhelm's *I Ching*, used the term "collective unconscious" to convey the same general idea.

2. Dao/tao: this is often translated as "the way," meaning the universal way, universal destiny but not in the deterministic sense, or one's personal path in life as both practice and process. It is also translated as "principle" or "truth." The Chinese character contains the symbols for "first or "primary" and for "boat."

3. This was written by the Persian poet Jawal al-Din Rumi (1207–1273) and is actually his poetical rendering of an earlier literary work, *Kashf al Mahjub*, by al Hujwiri. The poem is reproduced in the book *Traditions of the Prophet* by Dr. Javad Nurbakhsh, spiritual head of the Nimatulahi Sufi Order.

4. Taken from a talk by George O'Farrel in Santa Fe, New Mexico, in 1982.

5. Taken from a talk by Carol Bell Knight in Santa Fe, New Mexico, in January 1983. Ms Knight has authored two books, *Krishanta and the Way of the Avatar* and *Thought Has Wings*.

6. From the *I Ching* by John Blofeld, who is being somewhat critical of the *Ten Wings*, the commentaries attributed to Confucius but probably written by his senior students some time after the death of their teacher.

7. Michelangelo is best known for his fresco paintings and marble sculpture, but his poetry is remarkable in its own right.

8. From Carl Jung's foreword to Richard Wilhelm's *I Ching*, Princeton: Princeton University Press, 1950, page 45.

9. From Da Liu. *I Ching Coin Prediction*, New York: Harper and Row, 1975, page 7.

10. Martin Gardner, "Mathematics of the I Ching," *Scientific American*, January 1974, page 113.

11. The Nuclear hexagrams are a convenient way of dealing with interpreting the meaning or significance of a hexagram's central four lines. Only Hexagrams 1 and 2 have themselves as their own nuclear hexagrams.

12. These quotes are taken from Commentaries on the hexagram texts in Wilhelm's *I Ching*, pages 94, 98, and 170.

13. The hexagram names in upper case letters are the primary names used in this book The lower case names and those with an asterisk (*) are by Wilhelm. They are used here as a reference for those familiar with the hexagram names in his *I Ching*. Those names in italics are from John Blofeld's *I Ching*.

14. *Pinyin* is the current system of writing Chinese words in Romanization or Western letters. Previously the system of Roman letters devised by the scholar Wade were used. Wade used the spelling *tao* and *I Ching*. *Pinyin* spells the same words as *dao* and *Yijing*.

15. The original translation is: "it is rude and troublesome to appeal again and again." If you ask a question over again, even if it is reworded, you are actually inquiring about your doubt or dissatisfaction with the original response to your inquiry.

16. Wilhelm suggests you cast the *I Ching* again and translated this "inquire of the oracle [*I Ching*] once again whether you possess sublimity, constancy and perseverance; Then there is no blame." My understanding differs from Wilhelm's on this and addresses one's reason for casting the *I Ching* in the first place. My translation is: "When one's reason for [this] divination is fundamentally far-reaching and steadfastly correct, nothing is unfavorable."

Suggested Reading

Blofeld, John. *The I Ching*, New York: Dutton, 1968.

Blofeld, John. *The Road to Immortality*, Boulder: Shambhala, 1978.

Chan, Wing-tsit. *The Way of Lao Tzu*, Indianapolis, IN: Bobbs-Merrill, 1963.

Cleary, Thomas. (translation of Chih-hsu Ou-I), *The Buddhist I Ching*, Boston: Shambhala, 1987.

Cleary, Thomas. (translation of Liu I-ming), *The Taoist I Ching*, Boston: Shambhala, 1986.

Dhiegh, Khigh Alx. *The Eleventh Wing*, New York: Delta, 1973.

Govinda, Lama Anagarika. *The Inner Structure of the I Ching*, New York: Weatherhill, 1981.

Hendricks, Robert G. *Lao-Tzu Te-Tao Ching*, New York: Ballantine, 1989.

Hook, Diana F. *The I Ching and You*, New York: Harper and Row, 1973.

Huang, Kerson and Huang, Rosemary. *The I Ching*, New York: Workman, 1985.

Lau, D.C. *Lao Tzu: Tao Te Ching*, London: Penguin, 1963.

James Legge. *The I Ching*, New York: Dover, 1968 (1st ed. 1898).

Liu, Da. *I Ching Coin Prediction*, New York: Harper and Row, 1975.

Liu, Da. *I Ching Numerology*, New York: Harper and Row, 1979.

Lynn, Richard J. (translation of Wang Bi). *The Classic of Changes*, New York: Columbia University, 1994.

McKenna, Terrence, and McKenna, Dennis. *The Invisible Landscape*, San Francisco: Harper, 1975.

Moore, Charles. *The Chinese Mind*, Honolulu: University Press, 1967.

Schonberger, Martin. *The I Ching and the Genetic Code*, Santa Fe: Aurora, 1992 (1st ed., 1973).

Shaughnessy, Edward L. *I Ching*, New York: Ballantine, 1996.

Shchutskii, Iulian. *Researches on the I Ching*, Princeton: University Press, 1979 (1st ed., 1960).

Sherrill, W.A. and Chu, W.K. *An Anthology of I Ching*, London: Routledge and Kegan Paul, 1977.

Sung, Z.D. *The Symbols of Yi King*, New York: Paragon, 1969 (1st ed. 1934).

Sung, Z.D. *The Text of Yi King*, Shanghai, 1935.

Suzuki, D.T., and Carus, Paul. *The Canon of Reason and Virtue*, La Salle, IL: Open Court, 1964.

Waley, Arthur. *The Way and its Power*, New York: Grove, 1958.

Walter, Katya. *Tao of Chaos*, Austin, TX: Kairos, 1994.

Welsh, Holmes. *Taoism: The Parting of the Way*, Boston: Beacon, 1957.

Whincup, Greg. *Rediscovering the I Ching*, Garden City, NY: Doubleday, 1986.

Wilhelm, Richard. *The I Ching* (trans. by Cary Baynes), Princeton: University Press, 1950.

Wilhelm, Richard. *Lectures on the I Ching*, (trans. by Irene Eber), Princeton: University Press, 1979.

Wing, R.L. *I Ching Workbook*, Garden City, NY: Doubleday, 1979.

Wu, Jing-Nuan. *Yi Jing*, Washington, DC: The Taoist Center, 1991.

Yan, Johnson. *DNA and the I Ching*, Berkeley, CA: North Atlantic Books, 1991.

Young, Rhett, and Ames, Roger (translation of Ch'en Ku-ying). *Lao Tzu: Text, Notes, and Comments*,China: Chinese Materials Center, 1977/1981

Note: John Blofeld wrote the introduction to the book by Lama Govinda, who wrote the introduction to the book by Schonberger, who wrote the preface to this book.

hexagram chart

Qian,
SUBSTANTIVE   1.

Kun,
FRUITION   2.

Zhun,
INITIAL DIFFICULTY   3.

Meng,
INEXPERIENCED   4.

Xu,
PAUSING   5.

Song,
DIVISIVE   6.

Shi,
TEAMWORK   7.

Bi,
UNITING   8.

Xiao Chu,
HINDRANCE   9.

Lu,
AUDACITY   10.

Tai,
MERGING   11.

Pi,
SEPARATION   12.

Tong Ren,
RELATIONSHIP   13.

Da You,
PROSPERITY   14.

Qian,
HUMILITY   15.

Yu,
INSPIRATION   16.

Sui,
FOLLOWING   17.

Gu,
REPAIR   18.

Lin,
OPPORTUNITY   19.

Guan,
COMPOSURE   20.

Shi He,
BREAKTHROUGH   21.

Bi,
ADORNMENT   22.

Bo,
DOWNFALL   23.

Fu,
TURNING POINT   24.

Wu Wang,
NATURALNESS   25.

Da Chu,
FIRM RESTRAINT   26.

Yi,
SUSTENANCE   27.

Da Guo,
EXCESSIVE   28.

Kan,
FOREBODING   29.

Li,
ATTACHMENT   30.

Xian,
RESPONSIVE   31.

Heng,
ENDURING   32.

182

hexagram chart

33.
Dun,
WITHDRAWAL

34.
Da Zhuang,
POWERFUL

35.
Jin,
PROGRESS

36.
Ming Yi,
CONSTRAINT

37.
Jia Ren,
KINSHIP

38.
Kui,
STALEMATE

39.
Jian,
BLOCKAGE

40.
Xie,
LIBERATION

41.
Sun,
DECREASE

42.
Yi,
INCREASE

43.
Guai,
RESOLUTE

44.
Guo,
INSINUATING

45.
Cui,
ASSEMBLE

46.
Sheng,
STRIVING

47.
Kun,
ADVERSITY

48.
Jing,
SOCIETY

49.
Ge,
REVOLUTION

50.
Ding,
CIVILIZATION

51.
Jen,
PROVOKING

52.
Gen,
INTROSPECTIVE

53.
Jian,
PROCEEDING

54.
Gui Mei,
FORMALITY

55.
Feng,
ABUNDANCE

56.
Lu,
JOURNEYER

57.
Sun,
PERMEATING

58.
Dui,
PLEASURE

59.
Huan,
DISPERSION

60.
Jie,
LIMITATION

61.
Zhong Fu,
INSTINCTIVE

62.
Xiao Guo,
RESTRAINED

63.
Ji Ji,
COMPLETION

64.
Wei Ji,
INCOMPLETION

I Ching Hexagram Locating Cards

I have created a set of eight cards that construct and show the six lines of any hexagram and instantly identify the hexagram number, any changing lines, the nuclear and evolutionary hexagram numbers, and the nucleus. The cards make it possible to grasp the internal dynamics of change and transformation in the *I Ching* system and to better understand the nature of the subtle and often elusive permutations of change. The Hexagram Cards are not included in this edition for technical reasons. A limited number of sets are available and can be ordered while quantities last through www.artazzen.com

The cards make it easy to find hexagrams and to negotiate changing lines to another hexagram. When there is one changing line (as in Figure 25), the card is simply rotated upside down (inverted). The Changing Hexagram number instantly appears in the main window with the hexagram lines at the bottom left (as in Figure 26). When there are two or more changing lines, you can rotate them all to locate the Changed Hexagram. Or you rotate the cards individually, starting with the lowest. Each rotated card before the last change defines another Transitional Hexagram (page 64). These Hexagram Cards enable you to see and appreciate the real meaning and significance of changing the lines, one at a time. This way you experience the interim hexagram(s) that need to be passed through, understood, and dealt with between the starting and ending hexagrams.

By rotating the lowest changing line, you can see how it changes from one particular trigram to another, and to an actual interim condition that I call a Transitional Hexagram.

What is referred to as "Change" in the *I Ching* can more accurately be called transformation. Each change is actually a state (or stage) of transition in the continuum of our experience. Therefore we can think of the *I Ching* as a system of transformation and transition according to the yin-yang system and principles.

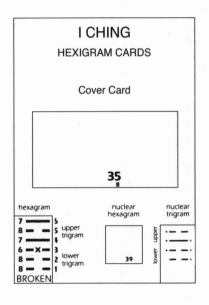

Figure 25

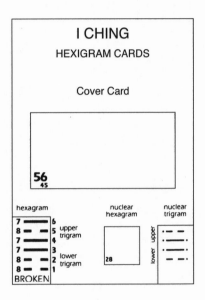

Figure 26

Trigram Upper → Lower ↓	KUN 0 ⚏	GEN 1 ☶	KAN 2 ☵	SUN 3 ☴	JEN 4 ☳	Li 5 ☲	DUI 6 ☱	QIAN 7 ☰
0 ☷	2 1	23 43	8 14	20 34	16 9	35 5	45 26	12 11
1 ☶	15 10	52 58	39 38	53 54	62 61	56 60	31 41	33 19
2 ☵	7 13	4 49	29 30	59 55	40 37	64 63	47 22	6 36
3 ☴	46 25	18 17	48 21	57 51	32 42	50 3	28 27	44 24
4 ☳	24 25	27 28	3 50	42 32	51 57	21 48	17 18	25 46
5 ☲	36 6	22 47	63 64	37 40	55 59	30 29	49 4	13 7
6 ☱	19 33	41 31	60 56	61 62	54 53	38 39	58 52	10 15
7 ☰	11 12	26 45	5 35	9 16	34 20	14 8	43 23	1 2

Figure 27. Hexagram Locating Chart

This chart is used to locate any hexagram by identifying its upper and lower trigrams. Locate the upper trigram along the row at the top of the chart, and locate the lower trigram in the column at the left. The large number in the box where they meet is the resulting hexagram number. The small number in the right corner is that hexagram's Opposite Hexagram (page 69). The ordering of hexagrams in this chart is the same as in Figure 1, the Fu Xi Square on page xii.

MONDO SECTER is a scholar of Chinese cosmology and philosophy whose work focuses on the application of *I Ching* principles to modeling culture and organizational cross-cultural (East/West) collaboration. He lives with his spouse, Ari Tomita, in Vancouver, B.C.